Japan and the San Francisco Peace Settlement

JAPAN AND THE
SAN FRANCISCO
PEACE SETTLEMENT

Michael M. Yoshitsu

Columbia University Press New York 1983

Library of Congress Cataloging in Publication
Data

940.53
Y65j Yoshitsu, Michael M.
Japan and the San Francisco Peace Settlement

(Studies of the East Asian Institute)
Bibliography: p.
Includes index.
1. Japan--Foreign Relations--1945-   -
-Treaties.   2. World War, 1939-1945-
-Peace.   3. Japan--Foreign Relations-
-United States.   4. United States--For-
eign Relations--Japan.
I. Title.   II. Series.
JX1577.Z5   1982   940.53'14   829662
ISBN 0-231-05514-5

Columbia University Press
87-2303
New York   Guildford, Surrey

Copyright ©1982   Columbia University Press

Printed in the United States of America

Clothbound editions of Columbia University Press
books are Smyth-sewn and printed on permanent
and durable acid-free paper.

CONTENTS

Preface.................................. vii

1. Early Planning for a Peace Conference,
    1945-1947............................   1

2. The Yoshida Initiative, 1948-1950.....   25

3. The Dulles-Yoshida Security Negotiations,
    1950-1951............................   39

4. The Price of Ratification, 1951-1952..   67

5. A Final Word..........................   99

Notes..................................... 101

Bibliography.............................. 109

Index..................................... 115

PREFACE

The San Francisco Peace Settlement capped the
first attempt by Japanese leaders to shape
foreign relations in the postwar period. During
seven years of Allied supervision, Tokyo officials regarded the treaty as something more than
a legal document restoring autonomy. In their
view, it was a diplomatic instrument that would
ensure survival after independence.

While crafting treaty policy, senior planners
looked to the United States for support of the
political, strategic, and economic provisions
that would bring lasting peace. In Tokyo, American preeminence among the Allied Powers signified U.S. leadership in implementing any peace
accord. Treaty success would thus hinge on a
new relationship with an old adversary.

The study that follows probes the ways that
Japan's post-treaty vision meshed with the
immediate goals of signing a settlement and
forging an alliance. For the purpose of clar-
ity, the study is divided into four parts.

Chapter 1 examines the first two phases of
treaty planning, when the concepts of peace and
diplomacy first emerged and were then trans-
formed. Perceived changes in Soviet-American
relations and U.S. strategic objectives, it
argues, changed a policy defined initially in
terms of diplomatic dependence on Washington to
one stressing military dependence on Washington.
Chapters 2, 3, and 4 analyze the next three
phases, reviewing how domestic opposition to a
prolonged Occupation, American demands for a
military buildup, and Japanese desires for ties
to Communist China created three new policies

whose goals were diplomatic equality with Washington and independent decisionmaking in Tokyo.

While the text discusses the international and domestic environment surrrounding treaty planning, it does not analyze them independently in great detail. Focusing primarily on Japanese decisionmakers, the four chapters consider how perceptions of domestic political protest, internal economic weakness, Soviet-American strain, and the like had an impact on treaty planning.

The view that emerges, therefore, depicts the San Francisco Peace Settlement as a series of five different decisions made in response to five different perceptions of the international and domestic situation. Taken as a unit, the decisions trace the steps that eventually led to independence for Japan and a new relationship with America.

Japan and the San Francisco Peace Settlement

EARLY PLANNING FOR A
PEACE CONFERENCE, 1945-1947

In November 1945 the Japanese Foreign Ministry
established an in-house committee to crystallize
thinking on a peace settlement. The need for
early planning appeared to be self-evident, for,
in Tokyo's view, the Allied Powers had pledged
to "make peace with a peace-loving Japan" once
the government achieved the goals of the Potsdam
Declaration [Nishimura (a)].

Although ministry officials assumed that peace
would eventually come, they were uncertain what
shape it would take or what their response
should be. Indeed, opinion within the government ran the gamut from support for a perpetual
Occupation to Japan's reincarnation as an American state [Hagiwara]. To clear up internal confusion, Foreign Minister Shigeru Yoshida asked
an old friend, Toru Hagiwara, to take charge of
the committee and give it policy direction.
Although at first Hagiwara hesitated, feeling
that his expertise lay in international finance
rather than international law, he soon accepted
the foreign minister's offer. During the prewar
period, Yoshida had supported Hagiwara's family
following the death of his father. Thus
feelings of indebtedness and loyalty to Yoshida
prodded the decision to help the foreign minister as his Treaty Bureau director.

In early 1946 Hagiwara and his assistants
began their study of peace against a backdrop of
rivalry between Moscow and Washington. Soviet
protest in the Allied Council to its excusion
from Hokkaido and to MacArthur's economic policies gave the impression of major power discord.
Nevertheless, the Hagiwara Group assumed that

regional tension would not prevent international
cooperation. After all, despite their political
and ideological differences, both countries had
successfully concluded peace treaties for Italy
and the East European countries in February
1947. The pattern of cooperation would presumably continue in the case of Japan [Hagiwara].
According to Hagiwara, "We expected the Americans and Soviets to work together on a peace
settlement for Japan. In 1946 and 1947 the
prevailing international mood was characterized
by great power tension, not bipolar estrange-
ment. We had not yet entered the cold war
period. Soviet-American relations seemed to be
on the chilly side, though. Perhaps we can call
it a period of 'chilly war'" [Ibid.].

While exploring the treaty issue, the Hagiwara
Group became more impressed with the need to
formulate treaty policy and devise conference
strategy as soon as possible. Statements by key
officials in the West seemed to indicate that an
Allied conference might convene sooner than
initially expected. In June 1946 Secretary of
State James Byrnes had issued the text of a
draft treaty proposing a twenty-five-year disarmament of Japan under a tight system of Allied
military inspection. Other officials, however,
reinforced the view that a peace conference
could precede an Allied withdrawal from Japan.
A five-year deadline set by Edwin Pauley for the
completion of the reparations program suggested
the intent to restore Japan's independence well
before a twenty-five-year period. And MacArthur's statements stressing the desirability of
a three- to five-year Occupation convinced
Japanese planners that an early accord was
likely.

Meanwhile, a mix of Allied statements and
domestic conditions suggested two props upon
which the Hagiwara Group could build treaty
policy.

In its view, the Allied Occupation was an American operation [Hagiwara; Takahashi]. Both Washington and SCAP had taken great precautions to support U.S. preeminence in Japan. America, for example, had appointed SCAP before agreeing to the creation of the Far Eastern Commission and the Allied Council, and had permitted the entry of British Commonwealth Forces on terms minimizing their impact in administrative affairs. More important, the United States seemed to stand alone as the center of the Western alliance.

Hagiwara and his assistants felt that wartime destruction had made Great Britain, France, and other Western Allies dependent on U.S. foreign policy [Ibid.]. And the Soviet Union, the strongest challenger to American leadership, had been effectively excluded from Occupation matters. To the Group's delight, MacArthur continued to oppose Russian demands for a division of command authority. As one official remarked, "The Soviets played dirty. They declared war on Japan after the atomic bombings of Hiroshima and Nagasaki, then annexed the Japanese territories to the north [the Kurile Islands], and subsequently forced Japanese prisoners of war to transport factories from Manchuria to Siberia" [Shimoda].

For the Group, American dominance over Occupation policy suggested U.S. leadership in ending its own administration of Japan. This first prop, American authorship of peace, led to a second prop regarding the American image of peace.

In 1946 and 1947 Hagiwara and his assistants focused on Washington and SCAP policy statements indicating the direction that an American settlement might take. The Group lacked inside knowledge about the Borton Committee, which had been established in October 1946 to produce a State Department draft [Hagiwara]. But its

review of newspapers and books resulted in an
estimate of peace that closely resembled the
document which would eventually emerge in Washington.

To the Group's alarm, America seemed to be
gearing up for a punitive treaty that could tear
apart the national fabric. Hagiwara and his
assistants were worried, first, about the possible severance of areas historically belonging to
Japan. In the Potsdam Declaration, the Allied
Powers stated that Japan's forceful seizures of
Korea and Taiwan had invalidated her claims to
them. Although the Hagiwara Group agreed, it
wanted Japan to retain sovereignty over the
Kurile, Bonin, and Ryukyu islands, which it felt
were parts of Japan proper. Unfortunately,
Soviet and American occupation of those areas,
and SCAP directives delimiting Japan's administrative control there, indicated Allied intent
to transfer Japan's legal title to the two major
powers at a treaty conference [Kawakami].

The Group feared that a move amounting to
annexation could spark nationalist sentiment and
flame irredentist passion. In its view, Allied
refusal to recognize Japan's rightful claims to
the Pacific Islands would not only strain Tokyo-
Allied relations but would perpetuate the threat
of a third world war [Ibid.].

The Hagiwara Group also worried about several
economic policy statements, including the Morgenthau Plan and the Pauley Report. It judged
that both documents sought to prevent future
conflict, with the former proposing the trans-
formation of Germany and Japan into agricultural
economies, and the latter calling for the removal of war-related industries from Japan
[Hagiwara; Shimoda].

To Hagiwara, both plans were "plainly ridicu-
lous" [Hagiwara]. The Treaty Bureau director
and his assistants concluded that Japan could
not survive under either scenario, for while the

nation had lost 45 percent of its territories,
it would have to care for five million people
returning from abroad. Only the revitalization
of trade, the Hagiwara Group felt, could prevent
economic collapse. It believed a trade takeoff
would solve the resource problem by giving Japan
export proceeds to purchase raw materials from
abroad, and solve the unemployment problem by
absorbing into manufacturing those workers who
could not find jobs in overcrowded rural areas
[Hagiwara; Shimoda]. In the Group's view, the
economic survival-trade equation held implica-
tions for industrial dismantling proposed by
Morgenthau and Pauley. Because these programs
would destroy Japan's fragile economic base,
some alternative policy would have to be constructed. In the Group's opinion, the logical
choice was a reparation of finished goods, not
of the equipment used to manufacture them
[Shimoda].

Finally, the Hagiwara Group worried about the
third component of a punitive peace: domestic
police restrictions. The Group clearly supported the demobilization of Japan's wartime
forces, but openly doubted the wisdom of Occupation policies decentralizing and disarming
Japanese police.

In 1946 and 1947, the Group feared the outburst of leftwing revolution. In its view, the
Japan Communist Party's role in organizing a
food demonstration on May Day 1946 and strikes
by railroad, coal mining, and electric power
workers revealed an elite committed to the
violent overthrow of government in Japan
(Ushiroku].[2] As one official recalled, "You may
be unable to imagine those early years when you
live in the present. Today, nothing really
happens when railroad employees go on strike.
But back then, the economy was in shambles and
the political situation was uncertain. In that
atmosphere, strikes . . . [and] protests were

foreboding, quite revolutionary. We felt that
the [Japanese] Communists were bent on toppling
the government, and that they would have suc-
ceeded had it not been for GHQ's decision to
clamp down on the labor movement and Communist
Party" [Nishimura (a)].

The Hagiwara Group were also concerned about
the negative impact that a surge in JCP activity
would have abroad. JCP-instigated attacks on
U.S. servicemen and street protests against
Washington's policies, it calculated, would
quickly erode America's willingness to help
Japan. The Group therefore felt that only a
large, centralized police force could prevent
the slide into diplomatic chaos and Communist
control [Nishimura (a); Ushiroku].

Hagiwara and his assistants responded to these
perceptions of peace with a policy two-step: go
American and stop a punitive settlement. From
the assumption of U.S. authorship, the Hagiwara
Group judged that Japan must attempt to influence Washington policy centers before a conference. In their estimate, early conveyance of
Japan's treaty position might protect the nation's interests at a conference that would
merely rubber-stamp U.S. wishes. The desirability of this strategy became more evident in view
of the Italian precedent. Allied negotiations
over that settlement in 1946 gave the Hagiwara
Group little hope of any Japanese influence at a
multilateral conference. Formal discussion of
the treaty went on without Italian participation
and, in that sense, resembled the Paris Conference of 1919, which had responded to a list of
German demands by refusing to recognize them.
The treatment of Japan, the enemy that had
fought the Allies two years longer than Italy,
would presumably be no different [Hagiwara].

Consequently, the Hagiwara Group decided to
relay its wishes through a set of "reference
documents." The strategy was simple: transform
national weakness into bargaining strength.
Papers dealing with the Pacific territories, the

national economy, and domestic security all reiterated the irreparable damage that harsh
treaty restrictions would inflict upon Japan.
The objective Allied interest in a peaceful and
stable Japan, the Hagiwara Group argued, would
best be served by a treaty that least burdened
an already overburdened government.

On the Kurile Islands, for example, the reference documents first offered a "scholarly
examination of the legal links between Japan and
that area." They referred to Japan's presence
in the southern Kuriles during the late eigh-
teenth century, and the Shimoda and Saint Pet-
ersburg accords (1855 and 1875), which recognized Japan's title over the island chain. The
reference documents next argued that the Ports-
mouth Treaty, ending the Russo-Japanese War
(1905), did not refer to the Kuriles; therefore,
Japan's sovereignty continued undiminished
[Kawakami].[3]

The documents then made a pitch for sovereignty with allusions to the "historic lesson on
the causes of war." On the Kuriles and other
Pacific territories, they stressed the government's desire to remain at peace with the world,
but cautioned the Allies not to repeat the mistakes of the recent past. Turning to Alsace-
Lorraine, the reference documents argued that
wrongful deprivation of territories had contri-
buted to the outbreak of the First World War,
and concluded that aggrandizement of Japanese
territories could again undermine peace by ig-
niting anti-Allied emotions which the government
would be unable to control [Ibid.]

With the drafting well under way, Yoshida
decided in February or March 1947 to communicate
Japan's treaty wishes to Washington. Wondering
whether the U.S. representative in Tokyo, political affairs adviser George Atcheson, would
agree to help, Yoshida, Hagiwara, and others
decided to try him on the Kurile Islands papers,
the first set of reference documents to be completed [Ibid.]

Yoshida apparently used Koichiro Asakai, of
the Central Liaison Office, to pass along these
documents. As assistant chief of the Tokyo
branch, Asakai had opportunities to attend
meetings of the Allied Council, an organization
established to advise General MacArthur on
Occupation policy. In 1946 and 1947 Asakai had
often met American and British Commonwealth
representatives George Atcheson and MacMahon
Ball to urge their support for an early settle-
ment.⁴ On March 12, 1947, though, Asakai met
Atcheson for a different purpose. During that
session Asakai offered an English translation of
the Kurile Islands reference documents [Kawa-
kami]. The American representative accepted the
documents, apparently regarding them as a statement of territorial wishes and not as peace
treaty preferences.
    Attempts to "open a window to Washington"
would continue that summer, but under a different leadership and different circumstances. On
June 1 a new government came into power. It was
headed by Socialist Party President Tetsu Katayama and supported by Democratic Party President
Hitoshi Ashida. As prime minister and foreign
minister, Katayama and Ashida assumed control of
a bureaucracy that fiercely opposed the new
coalition government's presumed leftist line.
In the Foreign Ministry, Vice Minister Katsuo
Okazaki and other senior officials seriously
considered resigning en masse. After some de-
liberation, however, they adopted a wait-and-see
policy. Apparently, fears of bureaucratic anar-
chy led to the decision to stay in office and
give the new government a chance [Nakajima].
    From the start, the Ashida Ministry formulated
policy in response to treaty signals emanating
at home and from abroad. In Tokyo MacArthur had
called for a Japanese settlement in the near
future. During a press conference the general
stressed Japan's readiness for peace, citing the

completion of military and political objectives
under the Occupation. Only peace, he reiterated, would ensure the achievement of the remaining economic goals. In his opinion, a
treaty would put trade "in the hands of private
traders . . . and return Japan's production to
self-sufficiency."[5]

After MacArthur's statement, members of the
Allied missions and foreign press in Tokyo told
Ministry officials that a conference might convene that summer or fall. On July 11 speculation turned into expectation of a quick accord
with the release of a State Department telegram
inviting all Far Eastern Commission members to a
preparatory treaty conference for Japan.[6]

To prepare for peace, Ashida studied the Hagiwara Group's reference documents and later mold-
ed them into an official summary of the government's treaty position. The contents of the
Ashida draft were not new, therefore, and, for
the most part, reflected the Hagiwara Group's
concerns over a punitive settlement.

The nine clauses of the Ashida draft collec-
tively aimed at mitigating treaty restrictions
which a U.S.-initiated conference would presumably impose. The territories clause, for example, asked for Japan's continuing sovereignty
over the Ryuku, Bonin, Kurile, and other Pacific
islands with the request for "careful consideration of the historic, racial, economic and cultural ties between those islands and Japan."

The two economic clauses equated economic
self-sufficiency and a decent living standard
with a treaty that would not impose further
restrictions in trade, shipping, fisheries, and
other key economic sectors. The political
clause requested that Japan be permitted to
undertake the obligations of a settlement without a post-treaty control or supervisory commission, while the security clauses supported both
a United Nations guarantee and the government's

prerogative to increase domestic police forces
proportionately to increases in population.[7]
Clearly, the Ashida draft repeated the Hagiwara Group's insistence on toning down any harsh
treaty restrictions. In that respect, it echoed
the earlier policy line and definition of peace.
But there was one difference. The foreign minister himself attempted to inform American and
European powers of the nation's treaty wishes.

In late July and mid-August, Ashida presented
the Japanese treaty summary to two American and
two Australian officials. The Americans were
the first, more important objects of Ashida's
interest, for, in his view, they represented the
government whose voice would command the conference and dominate treaty drafting. Ashida's
meetings with George Atcheson (political affairs
adviser) on July 26 and Courtney Whitney (chief
of the government section) on July 28 were more
than charges at communication; they were direct
attempts to influence American decisions on the
coming peace.

In the meeting with Atcheson, Ashida speculated that the political adviser would be recalled
to Washington to confer with U.S. leaders on the
peace conference and settlement. The foreign
minister also told Atcheson about a treaty outline that he had brought with him, and asked
whether Atcheson might transmit the document to
authorities in the State Department. The political adviser responded with the promise to
"take care" of the outline. After a brief
discussion over Soviet participation, Ashida
emphasized Japan's dependence on American good-
will in obtaining a satisfactory settlement.[8]

Two days later Ashida met General Whitney.
The Japanese minister offered the same outline
that he had given to Atcheson. The general
glanced over the document, remarking that SCAP
was thinking along similar lines. Whitney then
accepted the outline, while telling Ashida to

guard against public disclosure. News leaks
during that critical time, he warned, could have
unfortunate consequences for a settlement.[9]
   On the afternoon of July 28, Foreign Minister
Ashida received messages from the two Americans
requesting another meeting with him. During the
first session, the political affairs adviser
returned the Ashida outline, emphasizing that
his acceptance of it was not in Japan's interest. Atcheson, worried about Allied reaction in
the event Japan's treaty demands became public
knowledge, apparently feared an Allied boycott
in response to the appearances of a defeated
enemy dictating the terms of surrender and
American-Japanese collusion regarding the
course of a conference [Suzuki].[10]
   After hearing this explanation, Ashida tried
to persuade Atcheson to reconsider. He argued
that U.S. review of this "just and moderate"
outline could assist American drafting efforts
and help avoid the repetition of past mistakes
in which punitive peace later led to war.[11]
These explanations did not impress Atcheson;
when the meeting ended, Ashida left with the
outline in hand. The foreign minister then met
with General Whitney, who returned the document
for the same reasons that Atcheson had given.
   Several days later, Ashida visited the two
Australian officials to urge their backing of an
early conference and to inform them of Japanese
treaty wishes. Although Ashida viewed America
as the dominant power, he felt the support of
other Allies would be crucial to the success of
a conference. The foreign minister knew about
the British Commonwealth meeting scheduled for
late August in Canberra, where representatives
would presumably discuss policy toward a Japanese settlement. Contact with the two men who
would host the talks would thus be an opportunity to influence Commonwealth members before a
treaty conference.

On July 31, both Foreign Minister Ashida and
Prime Minister Katayama spoke to Australian
Foreign Minister Herbert Evatt. Ashida read a
prepared statement stressing the relationship
between an early peace, decent living conditions, and Australian-Japanese trade on the one
hand, and Japan's ability to exist as a peaceful, democratic, and unarmed nation on the
other.

During the meeting with Ambassador MacMahon
Ball on August 11, Ashida presented a copy of
the document that he had earlier offered to
Atcheson and Whitney. While glancing through
it, Ball asked questions about provisions for a
police force, reparations, and several other
items. The ambassador then accepted the document, while reminding the foreign minister about
Australian antipathy toward Japan and reaffirming his commitment to improve trade and diplomatic ties to Tokyo.[12]

Until the meetings with these Australian
officials, the striking feature about Japanese
decisions was the extent to which they paralleled U.S. treaty policy. Although unaware of
internal American planning, the Hagiwara Group
and Ashida Ministry had accurately gauged the
broad bases of State Department thinking on a
settlement.

In Washington the Borton Group pursued three
objectives in relation to a treaty. It first
worked to include the Soviets in a Japanese
settlement. Borton and his superiors believed
that an American refusal to cooperate with
Russia would cause it "to make things difficult
down the road." Indeed, Borton himself felt
U.S. acceptance of the Soviet presence in Sakhalin and the Kuriles was more desirable than the
antagonism resulting from U.S. protest. In his
view, the Allied Council, Far Eastern Commission, and other post-surrender organizations not
only provided for Soviet participation but also

served as valuable forums at which Russian representatives could blow off steam. American
planners thus assumed that cooperation could
prevent crisis, not that crisis had already prevented cooperation [Borton].

The Borton Group also sought to safeguard the
American strategic monopoly in Japan under the
guise of Allied cooperation [Ibid.]. On orders
from superiors, the Borton Group followed the
Byrnes disarmament treaty, which supported "a
dominant [U.S.] position in Japan in the days
following the adoption of peace."[13] It consequently proposed the continuation of a U.S.
military commander who alone would direct Allied
military forces in Japan.

The other clauses of the draft, a broad range
of territorial, economic, and security restrictions, indicated a final American goal of
keeping Japan militarily weak and peaceably
inclined.

Despite the Borton Group's efforts, State
Department treaty planning soon came to a silent
halt. On July 22 Soviet Foreign Minister V. M.
Molotov informed Ambassador W. Bedell Smith of
his country's opposition to a "conference of
eleven powers who are members of the Far Eastern
Commission." In his rejection, Molotov reiterated that the proper setting for Japanese peace
treaty review was the Council of Foreign Ministers, which had been "organized on the initiative of the U.S.A. . . . for the preparatory
work of drawing up peace treaties."[14]

Several weeks later, diplomatic counselor
Charles Bohlen analyzed the Soviet note and
radio comment for the State Department. In a
memorandum, he attributed Soviet opposition
to fear that the Yalta Agreement giving them the
Kuriles and South Sakhalin would be upset at an
eleven-power meeting at which they could be out-
voted. Bohlen then characterized the note as a
counterproposal rather than a rejection. To in-

duce Soviet attendance, the counselor recommended informing the Soviets of the validity of past
agreements and offering a change in voting procedure in exchange for Soviet participation.[15]
Secretary George Marshall agreed with Bohlen's
assessment and on August 13 sent Bohlen and
Llewellyn Thompson (chief of the division of
Eastern European affairs) to meet Soviet charge
d'affaires Semen K. Tsarapkin. Both Americans
assured the Soviet representative of the continuing effect of the Yalta, Cairo, and Potsdam
declarations, and in a second invitation
stressed that the rules of procedure would be
decided by the general conference.[16]
The Soviet Union then did the unexpected. On
August 29 it rejected the U.S. invitation a
second time. Marshall and other State Department leaders were stunned, for they had to
address treaty policy on the new assumption of
Soviet-American noncooperation. Complicating
this situation were China's strong opposition to
a Japanese settlement and Washington's own
unhappiness over the Borton draft [Borton].[17]
In early September, State Department leaders
responded with the decision to postpone a conference. In their judgment, delay would permit
them to discuss the Soviet response with Allies
rat the United Nations General Assembly and the
Council of Foreign Ministers meetings scheduled
for the fall and, more important, allow George
Kennan (of the Policy Planning Staff) to deter-
mine "whether it would be in [the] interest of
[the United States] to have a peace treaty with
Japan without Soviet participation."[18]
Because of these and other developments, Japanese leaders soon stumbled toward a redefini-
tion of peace that differed from the new position in Washington and past policy in Tokyo.
One trigger for change was General Robert Eichelberger, commander of the Eighth Army. On
September 5, Eichelberger met a close friend,

Kyuman Suzuki (Central Liaison Office director
for Yokohama), to inform Suzuki of his orders to
return to Washington for a review of U.S. security policy toward East Asia. In his view, the
trip's purpose was to help Pentagon officials
coordinate the withdrawal of Eighth Army troops
from Japan after peace [Nishimura (a)].

Eichelberger based his assessment on a narrow
reading of the policy environment. Because of
conflicting press reports and delayed communication from Washington, he looked to his superior,
Douglas MacArthur, for an indication of U.S.
policy toward Japan.

On March 19 MacArthur called for the start of
treaty talks in the near future, the withdrawal
of U.S. forces from Japan upon independence, and
United Nations supervision of the country following a settlement. The general further proposed, both within GHQ and to Washington, that
Japan's security be guaranteed by U.S. forces in
Okinawa and South Korea.[19] MacArthur believed
that an air force in Okinawa would be enough to
deter Soviet air and naval units that already
lacked sufficient fuel and numbers for an
assault on Japan.

Eichelberger strongly disagreed. He felt an
rair base in Okinawa could not replace U.S.
troops in Japan. As Eichelberger wrote in his
diary on June 27, 1947: "I can't see how they
can take troops out of Japan until the Communist
question is settled. We can't afford to let
Russian or Japanese Communists get control of
this country."[20]

Eichelberger again mentioned to Suzuki his
fears over American abandonment of Japan. The
general then asked his friend for an opinion on
Japan's defense needs after independence. A
brief statement, he apparently felt, could
strengthen his Pentagon case against Eighth Army
withdrawal. Startled by Eichelberger's comment,
Suzuki first asked for more time to consider the

request and then promised to return with something on September 10 [Nishimura (a)].

After the meeting, Suzuki informed Ashida of
the general's statement. The effect was electric. For the first time Japanese leaders had
been forced to confront Japanese security as a
live foreign policy issue. Until September 5,
the Ashida Ministry had defined peace as the
fight against a punitive settlement by America
and approved by all the Allies. The State
Department call for a preparatory conference in
mid-July had merely stepped up Japanese attempts
to convey their case for a liberal accord to
America and other power brokers.

In their view, external security was related
to Allied concerns over a future attack by
Japan. To assure Allies of their safety, Ashida
and his predecessors had stressed the sucess of
democratic reforms and demilitarization measures. The prevailing definition of external
security had therefore been defense against
Japan, not defense for Japan.

Another factor contributing to the leadership's lack of interest in external protection
was the assumption that American forces would
remain in Japan after peace. The Byrnes "Draft
Treaty on the Disarmament and Demilitarization
of Japan" had made a deep impression on Japanese
leaders. The document provided in part for an
Allied military presence that would oversee
Japan's adherence to treaty terms. Ministry
officials felt the term "Allied" to be a euphem-
ism for "United States." "After all," as one
Japanese observer remarked, "the Allied forces
during the Occupation were mostly American,
weren't they?" [Tatsumi].

Although Allied troops would ostensibly protect others from Japan, they could also effectively protect Japan from others. Apparently,
Ashida and his predecessors felt the Soviet
Union would not invade Japan when an attack on

U.S. forces would prompt an automatic American response.

Eichelberger's statement of pullout after independence shattered this security picture by removing the tripwire feature of U.S. protection. In a crisis atmosphere, Ashida convened the Foreign Ministry executive board to piece together a new security policy for the defense of Japan. On September 8, Katsuo Okazaki (vice minister of Foreign Affairs), Toru Hagiwara (Treaty Bureau director), Ichiro Ota (General Affairs director), Seiijiro Yoshizawa (Central Liaison Office deputy director), and Kyuman Suzuki first decided to offer Eichelberger a written opinion on Japan's defense needs [Nishimura (a); Suzuki].

The problem confronting the decisionmakers appeared to be a time constraint. Suzuki had promised to meet Eichelberger again on September 10, but a security statement would require a few more days. These officials therefore decided to seek a short delay by having Suzuki offer Eichelberger both a copy of Ashida's peace treaty draft and the promise to return soon with a statement on defense [Ibid.].

During the September 10 meeting, Suzuki mentioned his government's concern over Japan's post-treaty security. He further asked whether Japan would be permitted to build a small constabulary for domestic purposes, and handed Eichelberger the document which Foreign Minister Ashida had shown to Atcheson and Whitney.[21] Suzuki added that it dealt abstractly with the issue of Japan's security and would be followed by a more detailed description of Tokyo's defense requirements.

Although at first Eichelberger happily accepted the document, his mood quickly shifted. The general repeated his fears of a Moscow thrust southward which would follow the Eighth Army's pullout from Japan. Eichelberger mentioned that

Soviet forces in South Sakhalin and the Kuriles
could capture air fields in Hokkaido with impun-
ity, since nearby population centers would make
U.S. retaliatory strikes extremely difficult
[Nishimura (a); Suzuki].

After the meeting, Suzuki reported his conversation to the Foreign Ministry executive board.
Several days later the board made a series of
decisions which Vice Minister Okazaki reworked
into a Japanese security proposal. On September
12, Okazaki submitted the document to Ashida,
who had just returned from western Japan. The
foreign minister approved it and, evidently with
Katayama's concurrence, decided to offer the
proposal to Eichelberger as the "personal and
confidential opinion of Kyuman Suzuki." To
avoid the appearance of government initiative,
Ashida and Katayama had the proposal reproduced
on plain white paper, not official stationery
[Suzuki].

The desire for anonymity lay in the nature of
the document. Under this proposal, Japanese
leaders had abandoned their support for military
weakness in favor of strategic security. They
apparently felt that open government advocacy of
a pact aimed at protecting Japan against Soviet
assault would elicit unfavorable responses from
East and West. Both the Soviet Union and European Allies would be expected to oppose a formal
poposal suggesting an end to Japan's vulnerability. Protest against a bilateral military
arrangement would presumably be followed by
Allied withdrawal from a treaty conference and
Japan's greater isolation in a more hostile
environment. Ashida and Katayama thus judged
that private presentation of the Okazaki document would allow the prime minister to claim
ignorance in case of leak and escape political
fallout in event of diplomatic explosion.

On September 13 Suzuki presented his "written
opinion" to Eichelberger. The general accepted

the statement and later took it back to Washington with him [Ibid.].[22]   The document itself consisted of two separate parts with two different purposes. The first part advocated a United Nations guarantee of Japan's independence should Washington-Moscow relations improve. Ministry drafters included this clause not to express faith in great power harmony but rather to thank America for sponsoring a multilateral conference on the nation's behalf [Nishimura (a)].   The first part then ended with references to the threat of internal disorder and the need for a constabulary capable of dealing with it.[23]

The second part began on a different beat. It called upon America to defend the nation in the event U.S.-Soviet relations rapidly deteriorated. To cloak the strategic purpose of U.S. forces in Japan, Ministry officials proposed to justify them as units overseeing Japan's compliance with peace treaty terms. Japan could therefore reset the tripwire without having to acknowledge its existence.

Ministry planners also asked that American units be located in areas adjacent to the four main islands. Because Ashida and others had become weary generally of the Occupation and particularly of the U.S. military presence, they wished to relocate American forces--the symbols of Japan's subservience--to the Ryuku and Bonin islands. Although ministry officials viewed those areas as parts of Japan proper, they realistically felt the United States would retain control over them through some trust arrangement. In this sense, Japanese leaders used the legal fiction of continuing sovereignty to offer America areas which it already occupied and would eventually own [Nishimura (a)].

The second part also qualified the desire to keep American troops outside Japan. An "emergency stationing" provision would permit the reintroduction of U.S. forces into Japan upon an

actual threat to the nation's independence
[Ibid.]. By this provision, Japanese leaders
acknowledged that personal preference might have
to give way to military need.

Ministry planners ended part two with the
standard refrain for a stronger domestic police.
They mentioned MacArthur's direct intervention
that had checked Communist disruption and
thereby implicitly argued for an effective
constabulary after peace.[24]

Parallel to this new push toward security was
a new push toward peace. In August, Ministry
officials learned of Washington's second treaty
invitation and Moscow's second rejection. At
the same time, they were uninformed of the State
Department decision to postpone the conference.

Based on what they knew, Ashida and Katayama
first concluded that the Soviets would not
attend a Japanese peace conference. Before the
second Russian response, Ashida and his predecessors had never considered the possibility of
a non-Soviet accord. But after it, the foreign
minister and prime minister abandoned the
assumption of Russian participation.

In Tokyo, Ashida and Katayama took Washington's two invitations to mean a continuing
American commitment to an early peace. In their
judgment, the United States would simply pursue
peace on a separate, or non-Communist, basis.
Indeed, Ashida and Katayama's own feelings
supported this approach, for they strongly
wished to begin Japan's reentry into international society by ending the American Occupation. Failure to do so, they believed, would
continue "the American suppression of the Japanese spirit" [Suzuki]. Ashida and Katayama
therefore concluded that a conference should
convene without the Soviet Union, since Russia's
presence would introduce two-power conflict into
a diplomatic setting.

According to Kyuman Suzuki, "Foreign Minister

Ashida was very liberal, very broad minded . . .
an advocate of peace. He wanted to get along
well with America, the U.K., Soviet Union,
Australia, and all other nations. But [after
Moscow's second rejection] he judged a peace
treaty that included the Soviets was impractical
. . . that the Soviet Union and United States
would never come to terms at a conference. He
and Prime Minister Katayama therefore felt they
would have to settle for a separate peace . . .
one that excluded Moscow."

Ashida and Katayama of course realized this
policy would clash with JCP and JSP calls for
Russian participation. Nevertheless, they
estimated that widespread public support for
peace would overrule any demand for Soviet
signature [Suzuki]. As a consequence, they
began a quiet initiative for a quick accord.

Between September 19 and October 2, Ashida met
Assistant Secretary of the Army William Draper,
British Ambassador Alvary D. F. Gascoigne, and
Australian diplomat Patrick Shaw to ask their
support of a treaty conference.[25] Several weeks
later, Ashida, Katayama, and Suehiro Nishio met
Chinese Foreign Minister Wang Shih-chieh to
allay Nationalist misgivings about a Japanese
settlement. Katayama first informed Wang of his
determination to build a democratic society that
embodied the tenets of the new Constitution. He
then asked for China's backing at a conference.
Wang responded with a question, asking Katayama
whether the Japanese government could withstand
pressure from rightist and leftist groups once
Occupation forces were removed. Ashida answered
for the prime minister, but Wang judged Ashida's
assurances to be neither convincing nor
straightforward.[26]

After these attempts to solicit conference
support, Ashida and Katayama again tried to send
their treaty wishes to Washington. In early
November they apparently directed Chief Cabinet

Secretary Suehiro Nishio to meet acting political adviser W. Henry Lawrence. Nishio's remarks
are revealing because they show Tokyo's strong
expectation of an early accord and careful consideration of conference details.
Nishio first argued indirectly for Tokyo's
right to participate. In his opinion, a Japanese delegation would be needed to accept the
treaty terms that would be imposed on the nation. Such a delegation, he added, should be
headed by Prime Minister Katayama, who had been
chosen by 99-percent majorities in both Houses,
and it should also include the foreign minister
and leaders of the ruling and opposition parties.[27] Nishio next tried to stem American
support for an idea that had been raised domes-
tically--namely, a general election before a
treaty conference. He opposed the timing,
stating that candidates would base their cam-
paigns on the treaty issue. Nishio's superiors
apparently feared the politicization of peace
and a hardening of domestic opposition. Therefore, Ashida and Katayama had their chief cabinet secretary argue the adverse effects that
electioneering would have on the Allied Occupation. Finally, Nishio mentioned his belief that
MacArthur might represent Japan at the conference, and asked whether Japan could make its
views known to him before then.[28]
A few weeks later Katsuo Okazaki made another
attempt to gain U.S. consideration of Japan's
treaty wishes. On December 22, the vice minister offered the new political adviser, William
Sebald, a Japanese government study on the issue
of peace. Sebald turned it down as premature
but left open the possibility of acceptance
later when Washington might be interested in
knowing Japanese views on treaty matters.[29]
These low-level attempts to convey the
Japanese position were soon followed by a high-
level crisis. In December the magazine World
Report printed passages from one Japanese

document on a peace settlement. A related article referred to the paper as Japan's secret conference proposal and speculated that the former enemy would attempt to win more lenient treaty provisions by playing the United States against the Soviet Union, and suggested that the government would try to return Japan to "world power" status.[30]

The leak could not have occurred at a more inappropriate time. Five months earlier, Whitney had warned Ashida about the dangers of public disclosure. And three months before, Hagiwara had been forced to resign when The Pacific Stars and Stripes incorrectly attributed to him statements denying Japan's defeat during World War II [Hagiwara; Nishimura (a)].

Ashida sent Okazaki to apologize personally to Whitney and Sebald for the news leak. At the first meeting, Whitney expressed anger not at the fact that the Foreign Ministry had made a study of the treaty issue, but rather that it had allowed a disclosure to occur. He then gave Okazaki the impression that the Government Section desired "a thorough housecleaning" of the Foreign Ministry.

At the next meeting, Okazaki gave the government's explanation. He said the study had been one of several made to prepare Japanese representatives who might be asked treaty questions. Okazaki then mentioned the availability of only a few steel file cabinets in the Ministry and the difficulty of maintaining security there. Okazaki further said that the document in its entirety was innocuous and would have been considered as such if it had been accurately reported. He then expressed concern over undesirable repercussions that might result from the World Report version of the study.[31]

The two apologies were obviously not enough. Okazaki submitted his resignation in January, and the Japanese government waited patiently for the conference that would never come.

2

THE YOSHIDA INITIATIVE, 1948-1950

In November 1948 Prime Minister Shigeru Yoshida
started a second cabinet under the shadow of
treaty stall. As a member of the opposition, he
had supported the State Department call for a
preparatory conference and had been disappointed
by the Soviet response, which he branded the
cause of treaty failure [Nishimura (a)].
Although Yoshida lacked knowledge of Washington policy developments, he correctly forecast
the American decision to suspend its peace
offensive. In Washington George Kennan, the
policy successor to Hugh Borton, recommended
treaty postponement to his superiors at the
State Department. In Kennan's view, indefinite
delay would permit America to blunt the edge of
radical reforms that were strengthening an alien
influence in Japan. Kennan felt that the purge,
free speech, and other political and social
reforms were "uprooting traditional structure."
And he further judged that American demilitarization policies had left Japan more easily
swayed by the Soviets, whose forces were located
only miles away in the Kuriles, Sakhalin, and
Vladivostok. In Kennan's opinion, postponement
would permit America to rework these reforms,
strengthen the economy, and reverse the disarray
so conducive to Communist advance.
Throughout 1948 the Kennan recommendations and
their adoption by the Administration remained a
secret. However, the press presented in sharp
relief other factors that appeared to militate
against a U.S. pursuit of peace. From his reading of the environment, Yoshida concluded that
the Berlin blockade and the U.S. presidential
campaign had initially shifted American atten-

tion away from Japan, but that Nationalist defeat in China had sparked U.S. reconsideration
of East Asia [Nishimura (a)].

To the prime minister, that reconsideration
produced the decision to revitalize the economy
of a strategically more important Japan. Indi-
cations of this policy reorientation came with
public disclosure on March 10 and May 19 of the
Strike and Johnston reports. The two documents,
originally undertaken as studies of the reparations program, suggested a departure from Edwin
Pauley's call for economic weakness via industrial dismantling. The Strike report recommended that except for primary war facilities,
production facilities which could be used effectively in Japan not be subject to reparation
removal. And the Johnston report went a step
further, asking that primary war facilities
which could be used in a peacetime economy be
retained by the Japanese.[2]

The prime minister was pleased by this tilt
toward economic growth. Still, he had one
reservation. All programs seemed to assume a
prolongation of Japan's occupied status. In his
view, the American version of economic recon-
struction meant peacetime stability without
peacetime independence. But a perpetual occupation was unacceptable to Yoshida, for he felt
the restoration of Japan's independence to be a
matter of national honor and personal pride. As
one adviser related: "The peace treaty was
Yoshida's number one goal. He regarded 'de
facto peace' as an insult to the Japanese people
and ridiculed 'peace without a treaty' as a
'peace without peace'" [Nishimura (a)].

The treaty problem first confronting Yoshida
was, given waning support for a settlement
abroad, how to deal with growing unhappiness
over the Occupation at home. Fom late 1948,
Socialist and Communist Party Dietmen loudly
complained about Japan's inability to regain

national independence and bluntly asked the
prime minister when peace would come. In December Yoshida responded by pointing to the "objective situation" or "Allied disagreement regarding peace with Japan." In April 1949, Yoshida's
answers became more elaborate, but still sought
to place the blame elsewhere. On April 20, for
example, Yoshida noted improvement in Australian
and American attitudes toward Japan. He referred to recent Australian statements calling
for trade with Japan and American efforts to
eliminate job discrimination against Japanese.
Notwithstanding these positive developments,
Yoshida argued, American-Soviet strain leading
to treaty failure in 1947 had only intensified
after the Berlin blockade. In his opinion,
deterioration of the international environment
had made a difficult task even more difficult.[3]
Socialist and Communist opposition also raised
the security question in an attempt to embarrass
the government and attack its pro-American
alignment. In the Diet, they argued that independence and security could be guaranteed only
by total peace, political neutrality, and permanent disarmament, and asked the prime minister
whether he shared their support for an unarmed,
neutral Japan or favored a Pacific security pact
based on the North Atlantic Treaty model.
Yoshida occasionally mentioned his doubts
over their position, referring to Belgium, which
had been invaded[4] despite support for pacifism
and nonalignment. But to sidestep conflict, he
continued to refrain from commenting on a Pacific pact or other security arrangement. The
prime minister typically responded: "This is
not a concrete issue, but rather a concept. I
really have no right to mention my own thoughts
on this hypothetical question, since it relates
to security in the future. This matter should
be discussed[5] by the leaders who will conclude a
settlement."

From September 1949, after news stories reported the revival of U.S. interest in a treaty for
Japan, Yoshida and opposition attention turned
toward Washington. At the State Department Dean
Acheson, Walter Butterworth, and other key planners reconsidered peace in response to Japanese
unhappiness under U.S. rule. They felt the Japanese were becoming annoyed with "occupation interference with the minutia of daily life," "the
contrast between lush Occupation and poverty-
stricken Japanese living standards," and "the
usual number of atrocity stories involving Occupation troops." In their view, a manifestation
of the irritation seemed to be the dramatic rise
in Japanese Communist Party representation--from
four to thirty-five seats in the general elec-
tions of January 1949.[6] Although omitting the
reasons for treaty reconsideration, press reports signaled the near completion of a State
Department draft and U.S. support for some security arrangement with Japan.
    Embracing new optimism, Yoshida employed a
different combination of responses against his
Diet critics. From late 1949, he was asked by
Socialist and Communist interpellators whether
he favored a total peace that would include the
Soviet Union and Communist China or a separate
settlement that would bar them. The prime minister first cautioned that any decision regarding total or separate peace would be made by the
Allies, not by Japan. As he emphasized, "The
Japanese government is not in a position to express its wishes, let alone choose between
having or not having a total peace settlement."[7]
Suggesting that other countries might oppose a
treaty with Japan, he argued peace with a few
would be better than nothing and could eventually lead to a treaty with all.[8]
    As for security, Yoshida refused to answer
"hypothetical" questions regarding the U.S.-
Japan base arrangement mentioned in the press.

Nevertheless, the prime minister referred to
historic precedents in which a foreign military
force had remained to observe a host country's
compliance with treaty terms. Yoshida also
widened his area of legal maneuverability on
this issue, emphasizing that Japan possessed an
inherent right of self-defense "by diplomatic
and other means." According to this interpre-
tation, a base agreement could be justified as a
"diplomatic" measure that would not violate
Article IX of the Japanese Constitution. Though
Yoshida's answer was couched in ambiguity, its
purpose was clear: it sought to rationalize
acceptance of the Soviet-excluded, security-
oriented treaty which he believed America would
propose.

From late 1949, however, new developments
would force the prime minister to abandon his
wait-and-posture policy. In Washington, Secretary of Defense Louis Johnson and the Joint
Chiefs of Staff informed Dean Acheson of their
opposition to peace for Japan. On December 23
they argued that the Occupation would have to
continue, since instability in China, Taiwan,
and Southeast Asia made a pro-U.S. Japan vital
to Washington. In their view, undiminished U.S.
strength in Japan would best protect American
interests in East Asia.

Johnson and the Joint Chiefs did offer two
conditions that would make a treaty acceptable
to them. They would agree to support a settlement if the State Department could first obtain
Soviet and Communist Chinese signature to a
final accord. They reasoned that a treaty concluded without the Soviet Union, in particular,
would allow it to harass or invade Japan on the
pretext that the legal state of war had continued. The Joint Chiefs next demanded that the
peace treaty stipulate several security requirements, including the U.S. right to maintain
military forces in Japan and strategic trusts

over the Ryuku, Mariana, and Marshall islands.
Because the Soviet Union would never sign such a
peace settlement, Johnson and the JCS "reaffirmed their view that negotiations now leading
toward a peace treaty with Japan are still
premature."[10]
Acheson did not feel the Joint Chiefs' reasons
for opposition would present special difficulties. During an April 24, 1950, meeting, the
Secretary of State offered to meet JCS security
demands by supporting the right to garrison
troops and, if necessary, the right to move
freely in Japan. As for Communist signature,
Acheson argued that future Soviet actions would
be prompted less by legal considerations than by
existing political and power relations between
the United States and the Soviet Union
[Allison].[11]
In fact, Acheson agreed with MacArthur that
the Joint Chiefs, finding themselves in a militarily untenable position, were expecting to be
overruled on the treaty issue and would "cheer-
fully" accept Department demands. The greater
obstacle for Acheson was the erratic behavior of
Louis Johnson.[12]
Working relations with the Defense Department
rapidly deteriorated during Johnson's brief
tenure (March 1949-September 1950). The Defense
Secretary often complained about "do-gooders" in
the State Department and personally tried to impede the start of treaty talks. At one point
Johnson forbade members of the State Department
to discuss a settlement with Pentagon officials,
including General MacArthur. Dean Acheson and
John Allison later attributed the Defense Secretary's actions to the brain tumor that caused
his death [Allison].[13]
In Acheson's view, open confrontation with
Johnson would eliminate any possibility of peace
for Japan: "A public battle with Louis Johnson
over a wholly false claim that the projected

settlement neglected essential defense requirements, while appeasing the Japanese aggressors
and perpetrators of the Bataan Death March,
would be fatal to the treaty. It would be difficult enough to muster two-thirds of the Senate
to ratify a good treaty with Japan without
starting off a row within the Aministration."[14]
During the first half of 1950, the press
picked up the Washington impasse. One story,
for example, blamed the military desire to rearm
Japan in spite of Article IX, while another
cited General Robert Eichelberger's fear that a
treaty might permit Soviet bases in Japan. Despite inaccuracies, the reports clearly pointed
to Japan's strategic importance as the cause of
treaty breakdown.
Meanwhile, politicization of the treaty issue
in Japan had created a new set of pressures on
the prime minister. In October 1949 and January
1950 the Japan Communist Party stepped up attacks against a separate settlement. In publi-
cations, it warned that the government would
make Japan a slave to the Western powers, with
which it had signed peace, and an enemy of the[15]
Communist countries, with which it had not.
Several months later a group of Japanese in-
tellectuals, writing in Sekai (The World), also
came out against a separate peace. In their
statement, they argued that Japanese interests
would best be served by a total settlement, diplomatic neutrality, and United Nations member-
ship.[16] The Japan Socialist Party soon joined
in, calling for adherence to permanent peace and
neutrality and the withdrawal of foreign military units from Japan.[17] Following suit, the
Asahi Shimbun gave its editorial endorsement to
total peace, a United Nations neutrality guarantee, and the end of Allied base areas.[18]
In Yoshida's view, the "total peace" movement
did not threaten his electoral standing, for his
party enjoyed an absolute majority in the Diet

and he remained confident of his political position vis-a-vis the Socialists and Communists.
What worried the prime minister, though, was the
rise of anti-Yoshida, anti-American sentiment
throughout Japan and its long-term consequences
abroad.

Economic and strategic dependence on America
had sensitized Yoshida to the U.S. view of
Japan. As foreign minister in 1946, Yoshida had
feared that domestic Communist activity could
undermine Washington's willingness to help
Japan. And as prime minister in 1951, he would
order his chief cabinet secretary, Katsuo Okazaki, to apologize to the United States for May
Day demonstrations against Allied bases in Japan
[Nakajima]. Yoshida thus measured opposition
power in terms of the ability to undo an alliance, not to unseat his government.

Responding to this new situation, the prime
minister formulated a proposal which might end
the military-civilian stalemate over a settlement. In order to maintain secrecy, he worked
alone in drafting the document and opening a
route to Washington. Yoshida kept even Treaty
Bureau director Kumao Nishimura in the dark on
the coming initiative. This one-man approach to
high policy decisionmaking was typical of the
prime minister. According to Nishimura, it was
also desirable: "Yoshida was the right man for
those hard times. He was decisive, strong,
stubborn, and secretive. Of course, these same
qualities would make him less suitable for a
normal peacetime democracy. . . . But back then,
the times were tough and Yoshida was the sort of
leader that the country needed. You might call
him our version of Churchill" [Nishimura (a)].

The first problem facing the Japanese prime
minister was the route that a proposal might
take. In January or February 1950, Yoshida
decided to send Finance Minister Hayato Ikeda to
Washington. The purpose of that trip, Yoshida

originally thought, would be to arrange a meeting with Joseph Dodge (financial adviser to
SCAP). The prime minister intended to press
Dodge, through Ikeda, for a mitigation of Dodge
Line anti-inflationary policies that were intol-
erably restricting government financing and
overburdening individual taxpayers. Aware of
Yoshida's plans, the finance minister snapped
together an agenda and devised a negotiating
strategy for his talks with Dodge [Miyazawa].
But new developments regarding the peace treaty
caused Yoshida to view Ikeda's trip as a chance
to break the Washington deadlock. Despite this
change in purpose, the obstacle to the finance
minister's visit remained the same: General
MacArthur.

According to one official, "MacArthur viewed
himself as Japan's new emperor; he took responsibility for everything and refused to tolerate
interference from anyone." Yoshida consquently
worried that any attempt to despatch a ranking
bureaucrat to Washington would lead to the general's veto and undying enmity. To obtain
MacArthur's blessing for an Ikeda trip, Yoshida
said that the finance minister would study economic policy while in the United States. Supporting that objective, the general gave his go
signal to Ikeda's departure.[19]

Before the finance minister left, on April 25,
Yoshida told Ikeda to convey a personal message
on peace to some "influential person" of his
choosing.[20] The logical target seemed to be
Joseph Dodge. According to Kiichi Miyazawa
(then personal secretary to the finance minister), Dodge occupied a neutral position, serving
as an official in the State Department and adviser to the War Department [Miyazawa]. Other
considerations may have been Ikeda's familiarity
with Dodge and the unique position that he held
in the Administration. In the opinion of Ralph
Reid:

Dodge by this date had spent six to eight
months of the previous year physically in
Japan and had shown himself to be compatible
especially with Ikeda and Yoshida to the extent that he entered into financial matters.
I would say that Ikeda and Yoshida felt that
in Mr. Dodge they had found an individual in
Washington . . . to whom they could talk
frankly and personally. Dodge had the great
confidence of Ikeda and complete confidence of
Yoshida.

In standard Japanese fashion, I think, they
took advantage of a middleman, you might say,
who could represent them with all agencies of
the American government. With MacArthur they,
of course, had to keep a formal posture. Mr.
Dulles was an unknown quantity. They really
didn't know [Under Secretary of the Army
William] Draper very well [Reid].

After courtesy calls on General Robert Eichelberger and other military officials, Ikeda and
Miyazawa met Dodge and Reid on May 3. During
that two-hour session, the finance minister
broached the treaty issue. The personal message
that Ikeda would convey was a carefully crafted
combination of threat, proposal, and alternative.

Through his finance minister, Yoshida first
underscored the necessity of an early settlement. He stressed that opposition forces in
Japan had formed a united front calling for a
treaty on terms inimical to American interests.
These forces, he continued, vociferously opposed
a security treaty with America and U.S. military
bases in Japan.

Yoshida then raised another issue: Japanese
concern over American credibility. The prime
minister had Ikeda stress "that they [the Japanese people] had not forgotten the statement of

Secretary of the Department of the Army [Kenneth] Royall in February 1949 to the effect that Japan was not necessary to the United States. Emphasis had been given this by later public statements of the United States Government in writing off Formosa. It was further colored by the Communist gains in Indo-China, the fact that South Korea is not strong and could, perhaps, easily be abandoned, and that India's position is not altogether clear."

Yoshida next warned that the Japanese people were "desperately looking for firm ground" and hinted that they might turn to the Soviets, who, according to rumor, would offer a peace treaty stipulating the return of Sakhalin and the Kuriles to Japan. Only a peace treaty sponsored by America, Yoshida implied, could prevent internal chaos and undercut a separate Communist offer.

The prime minister, via Ikeda, next proposed a solution that would permit the United States to protect its security interests in Japan and enable Tokyo to have the peace that it desired. According to Yoshida, the Japanese government would invite U.S. military forces to remain in Japan, in exchange for the "earliest possible treaty" with the greatest number of Allies.[21] If necessary, the government would make a formal request for such a military presence.

In essence, Yoshida intended to overcome War Department objections to peace by offering it the legal basis for a post-treaty presence in Japan [Miyazawa]. Assuming that strategic concerns underlay military opposition to a settlement, he tried to assure military leaders that a treaty would not jeopardize the American position in Japan.

Realizing that this offer would have to play before a domestic audience, Yoshida made two requests that might mute public criticism. First he asked America to camouflage the security na-

ture of the U.S. presence. Tokyo and Washington,
he proposed, should conclude a formal agreement
stipulating that American forces would be in
Japan "to secure treaty terms and for other purposes."[22]   The prime minister then asked that
U.S. bases be made a "requirement of the treaty." This provision would permit the government
to deflect constitutional attacks with the argument that the treaty was an international agreement standing above domestic law [Miyazawa].
Yoshida could therefore assert that an accord
permitting U.S. bases in Japan superseded
Article IX prohibitions against "war potential."
    He then offered a policy alternative in the
event that a treaty proved to be unattainable.
Japanese discouragement over a treaty setback,
he contended, could only be offset by giving
Japanese more freedom in the conduct of their
internal economic and political affairs.
Through this general demand for "more freedom,"
Yoshida tried to establish a principle or objective that could be pursued in negotiations later
on [Reid]. If a treaty failed to materialize,
he continued, Washington should curb SCAP interference in the administrative phase of Japanese
law. As one example, Yoshida cited the Stabili-
zation Program, in which freedoms and decontrols
during implementation had been negated by low-
level SCAP interference.[23]
    Unless the Japanese government were allowed
greater freedom in conducting domestic affairs,
the prime minister warned, his administration
would continue to decline in popularity. If the
Yoshida government fell, no other party could
gain the working majority that it had carried
for the first time. The logic seemed to follow
that America would benefit from dealing posi-
tively with the Yoshida government, whose political position was secure and whose interests
paralleled those of the United States.
    Reid made a memorandum of the Ikeda-Dodge

meeting after consulting Ikeda, and later for-
warded copies to Butterworth and Dulles at the
State Department, Tracy Voorhees and William
Draper at the War Department, and MacArthur in
Tokyo.

Upon returning to Japan, on May 21, Ikeda
received a telegram from GHQ criticizing both
the prime minister and finance minister for
circumventing SCAP authority through direct
negotiations with Dodge. The message was ostensibly based on a Washington news story that
characterized Ikeda's meeting with Dodge as an
attempt to mitigate Dodge Line policies. The
underlying reason, however, may have been the
Reid memorandum which had been sent to
MacArthur.

After a noticeable cooling of relations with
SCAP, the prime minister sent MacArthur a personal letter reaffirming his recognition of the
general's authority in Japan. The apology
apparently satisfied MacArthur, for on May 25
the general replied that Ikeda's goals must be
accomplished within the coming year.[24]

3

THE DULLES-YOSHIDA
SECURITY NEGOTIATIONS, 1950-1951

The Soviet Union terrified Prime Minister Shigeru Yoshida. Moscow's decisions to scrap the neutrality treaty and seize the Kurile Islands seemed to betray Russian expansionist intentions, while the nation's military might and geographic proximity suggested the ability to carry them through. In the prime minister's opinion, only U.S. forces had deterred a Soviet strike southward against the home islands [Tatsumi].

For Yoshida, Japan's security clearly depended on a U.S. defense commitment. In 1947, the prime minister felt a de facto military relationship with Washington had already evolved. He then judged that Japan's educated population, strategic location, and industrial potential had impressed U.S. planners with the nation's importance, and later felt that East-West tension in Europe and over China had made Japan more vital and American protection more certain.

In Yoshida's view, Tokyo should shore up this strategic tie by supporting Washington's position in world affairs. A political orientation toward the United States, he calculated, would best consolidate the security interests of both countries against their common foe. A pro-U.S. posture could also avoid the military expenditures that he opposed. During the Occupation, Yoshida firmly believed that a Japanese counterforce would divert capital and impede recovery. In his view, long-term security required American protection and economic stability. Under different circumstances, however, the prime minister could have backed remilitarization.

According the Tatsumi, Yoshida would have favored Japanese armed forces in 1946 and 1947 had
the economy been strong and a military been necessary. Several years after leaving office, Yoshida wrote to Tatsumi: "The renewal of national strength and development of political independence require that Japan possess a military
force as a matter of national honor." In the
same letter, he mentioned his "deep feelings of
responsibility over the present situation on the
national defense issue." For Yoshida, opposition to remilitarization was relative, not absolute. And his rule that recovery must precede
rearmament would change with a changing economy
into support for a military buildup.

During his second Cabinet, Yoshida first anti-
cipated American pressure for rearmament. News
stories in late 1949 reported War Department
support for a Japanese military buildup. And in
early 1950, General Headquarters in Tokyo formulated a remilitarization plan for post-treaty
Japan. At that time Generral Charles Willoughby
(assistant chief of staff for G-2) felt Japan
would be defenseless if a treaty were signed and
U.S. forces were withdrawn. He told Tatsumi
that he had ordered subordinates to identify the
Japanese who might serve as officers in the
event an armed force were organized. According
to Willoughby, the list that resulted included
some four hundred names from the elite of the
old Japanese army school [Tatsumi].

From the press and Tatsumi's reports, Yoshida
judged that broad U.S. support for rearmament
would soon sharpen into direct American demands.
In June the State Department announced that John
Foster Dulles, then special consultant to the
secretary of state, would visit Korea and Japan.
The Washington representative, Yoshida felt,
would make a case for a military buildup while
in Tokyo.

Dulles would not disappoint the prime minister. Before their first meeting, on June 22,

the special consultant concluded that Japanese
rearmament was inevitable. According to John
Allison, director of the Office of Far Eastern
Affairs, "Dulles had an exaggerated fear of what
the Soviet Union wanted to do and was going to
do. He steadfastly believed the Soviet Union
was aiming at world conquest, and literally took
the proclamation by Joseph Stalin in The Prob-
lems of Leninism that the road to Europe is
through Asia. . . . The Sino-Soviet Friendship
Treaty [February 14, 1949] which seemed [to be]
pointed at Japan made him especially nervous"
[Allison].

Other factors underlying Dulles' support for
rearmament included his belief that the Senate
would never approve an indefinite defense commitment and his feeling that military dependence
would obstruct political independence. Despite
his conviction on rearmament, however, Dulles
did not then envisage a specific level of Japanese buildup. He evidently favored something
over 100,000 troops. But even this figure
resulted from "gut" feelings, not a technical
military analysis [Allison].

To deal with Dulles, the prime minister em-
ployed a strategy of contrived stubbornness.
During the first meeting, Dulles emphasized that
Japan would be strategically vulnerable after a
treaty. He repeated that only an arrangement on
defense could prevent Japan from falling to Soviet and Communist Chinese advance. The prime
minister's response was a mixture of ambiguity
and noncommitment tinged with sarcasm. In the
words of William Sebald, who accompanied Dulles:

Yoshida, as usual, spoke in circles and para-
bles; he refused to commit himself in any way.
The most he would say was that security for
Japan was possible, providing the United
States took care to preserve Japan's amour
proper [sovereignty]. Yoshida said that Japan
could have security if she demonstrated to the

world that she is democratic, demilitarized,
peace-loving. The world opinion would protect
her.
   Now, parenthetically again. These words,
incidentally, or much of these words were
taken from various policy decisions of the Far
Eastern Commission, and I think Yoshida was
sort of rubbing it in.[2]

After the meeting, Dulles became furious. He
fumed that the Japanese prime minister did not
know what was going on in the world and, according to Allison, kept up a temper tantrum for
quite some time [Allison]. Allison suggested
Yoshida's evasiveness may have reflected his
wish to sidestep a pledge to someone whom he did
not know well. Another explanation may be Yoshida's belief that he could best avoid rearmament through noncommitment and naivete. Such a
strategy could effectively elevate Ikeda's offer
of bases to the level of an implicit quid pro
quo: a U.S. right to garrison troops in Japan
for a peace treaty with an unarmed Japan.
   To enhance his bargaining position, Yoshida
gladly welcomed opportunities for Dulles to meet
opposition leaders, including Inejiro Asanuma
(Japan Socialist Party chairman), while in Japan. The prime minister apparently thought it
would be an educational experience for Dulles to
talk to leaders who completely opposed U.S.
bases in Japan and a treaty just with the West.
The effect of such discussions would presumably
be to underscore Yoshida's status as the only
reasonable Japanese leader in Japan. The chance
for Yoshida's further pursuit of these strategies was temporarily delayed, however. On June
25 North Korea issued a declaration of war upon
the South and on June 26 Dean Rusk advised
Dulles to return to Washington [Nishimura;
Allison].
   Three months later Yoshida again addressed the
security issue. But the circumstances had

changed. In mid-September news releases from
Washington indicated the end of War Department
opposition to a peace treaty for Japan. On September 14 the State Department announced it
would soon discuss settlement plans with Far
Eastern Commission members. And the next day,
Dulles outlined his conception of peace to the
press.

The Japanese response started off with a bang.
In mid-October, following the Washington statements, Treaty Bureau director Kumao Nishimura
and his assistants began to plan for peace on
their own initiative. Without direction from
Yoshida, they drafted a document analyzing the
American view of peace and recommending an appropriate government position. The paper that
they sent the prime minister ran against his
policy wishes. It supported total peace.

In 1950 Nishimura and other Treaty Bureau
members sympathized with opposition party and
press demands for relations with the Soviet
Union and Communist China. Moreover, they supported the anti-military spirit of the new Constitution that permeated the entire country.
And though they expected U.S. forces to remain
in Japan for a while, they felt United Nations
troops would eventually replace them as the
defenders of peace [Nishimura (a)].

After reading the document, Yoshida angrily
rejected the Treaty Bureau's calls for Communist
signature and United Nations security. According to Nishimura, "His [the prime minister's]
face turned bright red when he saw what we were
proposing. . . . Yoshida [then] raked me over
the coals for supporting the bankrupt position
of the opposition parties, and told me to come
up with a more realistic draft."[3] Through sheer
force of personality, the prime minister thus
rerouted policy planning along a new separate-
treaty track. As another official wryly remarked, "Mr. Yoshida could be a very frightening,
very persuasive individual" [Fujisaki].

On December 27, 1950, the Treaty Bureau completed the separate peace treaty draft that Yoshida had demanded, and on December 28 presented
it to the prime minister. They reworked the
document in mid-January 1951 and, in response to
Yoshida's request, prepared a summary for presentation to him on January 20.

The treaty draft that had emerged in late December reflected Yoshida's support for security
based on a pro-American orientation. The document contained several standard provisions, including the restoration of full independence,
the right of internal defense, and the omission
of economic restrictions.[4] It also had something new--namely, the conclusion of a bilateral
peace settlement between the United States and
Japan. Yoshida's talk had apparently persuaded
Nishimura and his assistants to view the participation of other nations as a "purely academic
matter." According to one bureau member, they
soon concluded that the Pacific war had been
fought between these two countries; therefore, a
treaty with America would end the state of bel-
ligerency with the only power that mattered
[Takahashi].

The bureau also judged that the two-party
signature could more quickly align Japan with
America. In its opinion, Australia and other
"anti-Japanese" Allies would oppose the liberal
accord that America seemed to support. But
bureau members felt these Allies needed U.S. aid
and protection to survive. In their view, a bilateral treaty would not only exclude opponents
from the treaty process but would force their
eventual support for a U.S.-sponsored agreement.

The treaty draft included a final provision on
an issue which Yoshida felt could unravel the
Japan-U.S. relationship. He strongly believed
the Pacific islands to the north and south were
part of Japan. And he feared that a U.S. trus-
teeship, particularly over the Ryukus and Bon-

ins, would sever them and ignite irredentism and
anti-Americanism throughout Japan. Yoshida approved the bureau recommendation for a United
Nations Security Council decision on the fate of
the Soviet-held Kuriles. But he asked for a
different proposal on the Ryukus and Bonins,
where the United States had control and the
chance of reversion seemed to be greater. In
compliance with Yoshida's request, Nishimura and
the bureau formulated several alternatives, including a Bermuda-type lease arrangement that
would ensure U.S. control while recognizing
Japan's nominal ownership claims. Yoshida and
the bureau judged that this plan would alleviate
domestic fears regarding territorial loss without jeopardizing the American strategic position
in East Asia [Nishimura (a)].

After giving his instructions for a peace
treaty, Yoshida informed Nishimura of the security treaty that he wanted. In mid-October, the
prime minister indicated his interest in a document that would establish a Japan-U.S. collective self-defense relationship and permit an
American presence in Japan. By this draft, Yoshida intended to obtain a U.S. defense commitment for an unarmed Japan.[5] A base offer, he
felt, was his best bargaining chip.

Yoshida believed that Japan's strategic importance to America had risen quickly after the
North Korean attack on the South. He therefore
tried to use Japan's elevated status to strengthen his negotiating position with America. On
July 29 the prime minister withdrew his May 3
offer to Joseph Dodge of U.S. bases in Japan for
the "earliest possible treaty." Appearing before the Upper House Foreign Affairs Committee,
Yoshida affirmed his opposition to a foreign
military presence and denied reports that the
Allies had requested base rights in Japan.

Three days later Vice Minister of Foreign Affairs Ichiro Ohta met William Sebald to repeat

the prime minister's opposition to Allied bases.
When asked about Japanese security expectations,
the vice minister replied that Japan, like the
Republic of Korea, would rely on the United Nations for protection.
Several days later Sebald sent his assessment
of the Yoshida statement to Washington. In his
view, it represented an attempt to lay. the
groundwork for future bargaining with the United
States on a peace settlement. The State Department agreed. On August 29 Marshall Green, of
the Office of Northeast Asian Affairs, wrote:

> The war in Korea has pointed up the need for
> US bases in Japan. Just as US bases made it
> possible for the US to go to the defense of
> South Korea, so it is now clear that US bases
> in Japan will prove a critical factor in pro-
> tecting the whole US position in the Far East.
> Japanese leaders must be fully aware of this
> fact, and it would be logical for the Japanese
> (who have never hesitated to play power poli-
> tics on a grand scale) to intimate that the
> price for these all-important bases in Japan
> is greater than the US had perhaps reckoned.
> . . . Because acceptance of US bases is the
> price Japan knows she must pay for an early
> treaty, Mr. Yoshida is probably prepared to
> accept them at least for a defined short per-
> iod of time, provided the other treaty terms
> and supplementary concessions (such as econ-
> omic aid) are adequate.[6]

With the end of Defense Department opposition
to a treaty, Yoshida turned his attention in
September from early peace to a security accord.
Although the policy objective changed, the tool
of persuasion remained the same.
Treaty Bureau members working on Japan's military proposal also felt bases were important.
Unlike Yoshida, though, they linked their assessment to events in Washington, not Korea.

Nishimura and his assistants judged that the
Pentagon supported a treaty because Dulles had
pledged that peace would not disturb the strategic status quo in Japan. They felt this promise
had placed Dulles in a difficult position. In
their view, Dulles could not directly demand a
partial surrender of Japanese sovereignty for
security purposes; normally, he would have to
wait for the prime minister to broach the subject of bases. But Dulles could try to raise
the issue indirectly by asking Yoshida about his
security views. At that time,Yoshida could man-
ipulate Dulles' presumed indebtedness to the
Pentagon to Japan's advantage. He could offer
base areas in exchange for U.S. support of an
unarmed Japan and a collective self-defense relationship tied to the United Nations Charter
[Fujisaki].
  The first demand flowed from Yoshida's instructions regarding nonrearmament. But the
second demand resulted from the bureau's own
perception. Nishimura and his assistants worried that a formal military agreement with America could stimulate stronger antigovernment sentiment. They believed that a security treaty
would be more acceptable to the Japanese people
if cast in the mold of the United Nations, an
international organization for world peace. The
government could thus justify U.S. forces in
Japan as a regional security arrangement established under United Nations auspices.
  A security treaty reference to the Charter,
the bureau also calculated, could minimize Article IX objections to an American military presence. The government could argue that the Japanese Constitution must follow the principles of
international law. Therefore, the Yoshida Administration and Japanese people would have to
accept U.S. bases as a duty under the most basic
international agreement, the UN Charter. In
this manner, the bureau could avoid Article IX

by linking Japanese responsibilities to international legal obligations [Nishimura (a)].

Finally, the bureau favored reference to a "collective self-defense relationship" in order to emphasize an equal partnership between Japan and America. Nishimura and his assistants shared a sense of personal frustration over Japan's subordinate position to the United States and feared domestic opposition to a one-sided security arrangement. They felt some reference to a collective self-defense relationship would permit the government to claim that U.S. actions followed Japanese wishes and that differences of opinion could be settled through open discussion [Takahashi].

Nishimura and other bureau members, however, placed a practical limit on their desire to project an image of mutuality in Japan-U.S. relations. This limit surfaced during a debate over a proposal made by Masato Fujisaki. As Treaty Bureau section chief, Fujisaki worried about adverse domestic reaction to a one-sided security accord. In his view, the U.S.-Philippine base agreement constituted a humiliating surrender of Philippine sovereignty to the United States. To avoid a repetition of that precedent, Fujisaki suggested, Japan should sign a peace treaty, wait for an unspecified length of time, and then sign the security treaty with America. The delay, he asserted, would give the people the impression that an independent government had freely and deliberately chosen to conclude the document. According to the section chief, a security treaty signed together with the peace treaty would be vulnerable to the criticism of having been forced on Japan by the United States; opposition parties could charge that America had twisted Japan's desire for peace into acceptance of an unwanted base arrangement [Fujisaki].

Other Treaty Bureau members dug in their heels against Fujisaki. They feared that a delay in

Japan's security treaty signature might jeopardize the chances for a peace settlement. Parties out of power, for example, could be expected to support the peace settlement and oppose
any security arrangement. But America would
never agree to one without the other. Thus,
bureau members minus Fujisaki assumed that the
government would sign the two treaties together
and then submit them to the Diet, as a fait ac-
compli, to be accepted or rejected as one legislative package [Ushiroku]. In their view, the
practical need to conclude treaties of peace and
security would have to override the "niceties"
of equal appearance and domestic acceptability.
Fujisaki lost. His recommendation never reached
the prime minister.

After this debate, Yoshida ordered the Treaty
Bureau to produce a second security treaty
draft. In the prime minister's words, "The
peace treaty negotiations must proceed along the
premise of an unarmed Japan. As a consequence,
we may have to offer some ideal plan calling for
demilitarization or military restrictions."

Under instructions from Yoshida, Nishimura
drafted "A Proposal for the Advancement of Peace
and Security in the Northern Pacific Region"
with assistance from Tatsumi. The director drew
up the general framework of the document, while
Tatsumi filled in the details on geographic location and armed forces [Nishimura (b)]. The
document that emerged in late December, 1950,
proposed limiting British, Soviet, and Chinese
military units to levels needed for external
security and establishing a demilitarized zone
in the Far East. In the opinion of Fujisaki,
the basis of this security treaty may have been
MacArthur's earlier call to transform Japan into
the Switzerland of the Far East--that is, a
country whose neutrality and integrity would be
guaranteed by the United Nations [Fujisaki].

Yoshida apparently formulated the basic
components of the proposal alone. On several

occasions, he met Tatsumi and other former military officers before ordering Nishimura to draft the document. Those discussions consisted of Yoshida's questions about the efficacy of such an arrangement rather than a think-through process leading to it. In fact, Yoshida's suggestions for a Far Eastern demilitarized zone and an unarmed Japan appalled Tatsumi and the others [Tatsumi].

The Treaty Bureau director conceded the fancifulness of the proposal. In an interview, Nishimura suggested that Yoshida had had the document prepared in order to have an alternative security arrangement "in the event direct negotiations necessitated its presentation" [Nishimura (a)]. This would presumably coincide with America's rejection of Yoshida's first security proposal and result in U.S. reconsideration of that more realistic draft.

The opportunity to test bargaining strategies would come soon. On January 11, 1951, the State Department announced that Dulles would confer with General MacArthur and Japanese leaders on a peace settlement. Two weeks later the special consultant arrived in Tokyo. To set the stage for the coming talks, John Allison and William Sebald personally gave the prime minister a memorandum on the "Seven Principles of Peace" and a thirteen-point agenda for his review. Yoshida responded by ordering the Treaty Bureau to draft both a general statement supporting the Seven Principles' call for early peace and several articles stating the Japanese position on the proposed agenda.[8]

On January 29, Dulles and Yoshida started their first meeting. In opening remarks, the two men exchanged wishes for a liberal accord and lasting peace. Dulles noted that the settlement would have been a harsh document had it been signed three years earlier. But in 1951 the Allies wanted to make peace with Japan as

one friend to another, not as victor to the van-
quished.[9] For his part, Yoshida stressed his
interests in establishing a democratic, self-
sufficient country that could assist the free
world, and in ending administrative controls
that ignored Japanese reality and threatened
friendly relations with America.
  The discussion then changed. In a succession
of verbal bursts, Dulles redirected the conversation to the subject of Japanese rearmament.
He chided Yoshida for advocating the restoration
of independence without specifying what contribution Japan would make after independence.
Dulles repeated his point that political autonomy carried with it the moral obligation to
assist the free world, and then asked Yoshida
how Japan intended to make a contribution in
event of war.[10]
  The prime minister began his response in a
roundabout manner. He first said that Dulles'
reference to a "contribution" probably signified
his wish to know Japanese intentions on rearmament. Yoshida emphasized that a discussion of a
post-treaty contribution was premature. In his
view, the most pressing issue was the restoration of independence; when that occurred, Japan
would be willing to consider a contribution.[11]
  The prime minister, openly scoffing at the
idea of Japanese rearmament and bluntly telling
Dulles that he must be joking, argued that rearmament would impede economic recovery and
stimulate the rebirth of a prewar military
elite. Nevertheless, Yoshida hoped Washington
would still regard Japan as a country falling
within the American orbit.[12]
  Dulles became upset at Yoshida's response. He
interpreted it as naive and an indication of the
prime minister's desire to give bargaining hints
but unwillingness to discuss broad principles.[13]
  When the meeting ended, at 6:00 p.m. both
representatives went to see General MacArthur.

During the discussion, MacArthur agreed that rearmament would be inappropriate and suggested a
military contribution of the old arsenals and
idle facilities belonging to the Japanese army
and navy. MacArthur contended this policy would
help the United States, whose own armament program had been delayed, and also provide a boost
to the Japanese economy. The general concluded
with the promise to send Dulles a copy of his
investigation into the arsenals and facilities
that might be used by the United States in
Japan.[14]

Despite MacArthur's remarks, Dulles remained
unconvinced about the virtues of an unarmed
Japan. At an American staff meeting the next
day, he expressed pessimism over Yoshida's attitude and evidently had Sebald tell the prime
minister to stop stalling.[15]

In Dulles' view, events in Korea clearly over-
rode the general's objections to Japanese rearmament. He felt that the North Korean attack in
late June signaled a Soviet attempt to contol
the manpower and industrial resources of Japan
and that such control over Japan and Germany
would permit the Soviet Union to sustain and win
a long war against America. In Dulles' estimate, in fact, the difficulty with Japan was its
distance from the United States and its proximity to the Soviet Union. America, Dulles believed, could not protect Japan singlehanded.
It would need help from the Japanese.[16]

Communist China's intervention five months
later only made a bad situation worse. On November 30, 1950, Dulles wrote, "Developments in
Asia confirm that there is a comprehensive program, in which the Soviets and Chinese are coop-
erating, designed in a present phase to eliminate all Western influence on the Asiatic mainland, and probably also in relation to the islands of Japan, Formosa, the Philippines, and
Indonesia."

One way to deal with the new Sino-Soviet
threat, Dulles proposed, was to use Taiwan "as a
base for covert and perhaps open Chinese activities against the China mainland, which would at
least divert the Chinese communist government."
In addition, Dulles mentioned the "possibility
of stimulating guerrilla and insurrectional activities in China against the Communist government" and "stepping up subversive activities
within areas of Soviet contrrol, wherever there
are any elements available for such purposes."
He continued, "Our best defense lies in exploit-
ing potential jealousies, rivalries, and disaf-
fections with the present area of Soviet communist control so as to divert them from external
advantages to the problem of attempting to consolidate an already overextended position."
    For long-term security, Dulles favored a Paci-
fic Pact, which he had opposed before the Korean
War. In April 1950 he felt a formal arrangement
would commit stronger and more responsible nations to support unstable and irresponsible members, and would suggest to the Communists that
they could expect no U.S. opposition in countries excluded from the arrangement. But the
North Korean attack and Communist Chinese intervention changed the strategic ballgame. In his
view, U.S. security interests required a Pacific
Pact composed "initially of Japan, Australia,
New Zealand, the Philippines, the United States
and perhaps Indonesia." In the first phase the
military support of Australia and New Zealand,
"the only two dependable countries in the Pacific area," would be vital to the success of this
security web.[17]
    Meanwhile, the United States should commit
sea, air, and land units to the defense of
Japan, pending the development of some land
force of their own. Dulles felt that a tie between Japanese military units and a Pacific Pact
would minimize domestic opposition to a Tokyo

defense effort. In his view, the Korean situation had awakened Japan from her postwar stupor. But he believed the Japanese people still opposed rearmament and would accept bases only as a necessary last resort for defense. Dulles judged that a Pacific Pact, authorized by Article 51 of the United Nations Charter, would internationalize Japanese forces and thus "ease reconciliation with the present . . . Constitution."[18]

A second meeting with Yoshida, on January 31, 1951, did not alter Dulles' assessment. In one respect, the U.S. representative actually displayed a tougher attitude on defense. To Yoshida's dismay, he rejected Japan's request for a Bermuda-style lease arrangement over the Ryuku and Bonin islands, reasserting that they would go to America under a strategic trust arrangement. The United States, Dulles argued, had no reason to consider Japanese wishes regarding the sovereignty of those areas [Nishimura (a)]. After that session, Dulles decided to press Yoshida indirectly on rearmament. The forum would be staff-level talks set for February 1 and 2.

Before entering those discussions, Japanese officials clearly occupied a weaker-than-expected bargaining position, for Yoshida and the Treaty Bureau had overestimated the utility of bases. The prime minister assumed that these facilities were vital to U.S. interests in the Far East, and concluded that the right to maintain "strategic dispositions" would elicit Dulles' acceptance of an unarmed Japan.

But the U.S. representative had a different view. He defined American security in terms of a Japanese promise to rearm, and assumed a peace settlement would permit the United States to keep bases in Japan and have control over the Ryukus and Bonins.

As for the Treaty Bureau, Nishimura and his assistants had earlier judged that Dulles won

military support for a treaty after promising
the Pentagon base rights in post-treaty Japan.
In their opinion, Yoshida could twist this indebtedness to stop a Dulles rearmament charge.
The defense secretary and Joint Chiefs, however,
withdrew their opposition for a different
reason.
    In late August, 1950, Acheson instructed Alli-
son to agree to several treaty conditions which
the Pentagon had made the price of its support.
Both men had strongly opposed these stipula-
tions, particularly the provisions delaying a
treaty until victory in Korea, denying Japanese
resources to the Soviet Union, and declaring
Japan's right of self-defense. They felt that
these requirements were so bluntly stated as to
be unacceptable to Japan and all noncommunist
Allies. Acheson and Allison also believed many
of the provisions had been met elsewhere in the
State Department's peace treaty draft. Despite
their reservations, they viewed acceptance of
them as the only way to start the movement toward peace. After bringing the Pentagon into
negotiations, they felt that the military would
eventually realize the impossibility of achiev-
ing all security requirements in a peace treaty
with Japan [Allison].
    Three months later, the State Department
backed away from these concessions without
losing Pentagon support. The reason was a new
secretary of defense. After assuming office,
George Marshall consistently supported Administration policy in spite of JCS unhappiness.
Acheson, Allison, and Dulles could therefore
pursue peace with a free hand.
    The prime minister made a second miscalcula-
tion of his bargaining strength. In 1951, Yoshida assumed MacArthur would be an important
ally on the rearmament issue. The general's
strong opposition to Japanese military forces
was well known within Japanese and American

planning circles. During his meeting with
George Kennan (March 1948), MacArthur had opposed a military buildup, citing domestic opposition, financial cost, and Allied fears.[19]   By
1951 he had revised his thinking somewhat, re-
versing his prior opposition to U.S. bases and a
well-equipped Japanese police force. Despite
these changes, MacArthur still felt uneasy over
Japanese rearmament.

Aware of the general's views, Yoshida apparently met MacArthur in mid-January, 1951, to
form a "secret alliance." He first mentioned
his belief that Dulles would again ask Japan to
rearm. The prime minister then said that military overspending had once led to economic collapse and stressed that financial considerations
would constrain another major arms buildup.
MacArthur agreed and offered to support Yoshida
against Dulles.[20]

Yoshida's mistake was the assumption that the
general could persuade Dulles. During a State
Department meeting on April 5, Dulles expressed
concern about MacArthur and the phenomenon of
"localitis." According to Dulles, General Lucius Clay in Germany and other U.S. commanders
abroad judged Washington proposals on the basis
of local popular support.[21]   Dulles felt MacArthur must be consulted for his views on a settlement. Nevertheless, the general must not be
allowed to veto items vitally affecting the
American national interest. In Dulles' estimate, Japanese rearmament was clearly one such
element.

Finally, Yoshida misjudged Dulles himself.
According to Nishimura, Japanese representatives
should have been prepared to make a rearmament
concession before entering staff-level talks.
In his opinion, the prime minister should have
perceived the need to compromise on rearmament
during his two meetings with Dulles. Because of
his lack of facility with spoken English, Yoshi-

da apparently underestimated Dulles' desire on
this issue. Whether for secrecy or pride as the
former ambassador to Great Britain, he chose not
to use an interpreter when he met Dulles. Evidently, deteriorating conversational skills
caused the prime minister to miss the pitch and
fervor of the American's rearmament demands
[Nishimura (b)].

Because of these misperceptions, Japanese
officials started off staff-level talks with an
inaccurate fix on their bargaining position. On
February 1, Foreign Affairs Vice Minister Sadao
Iguchi and Treaty Bureau director Kumao Nishimura gave the American delegates their version
of a security treaty.

The U.S. representatives, John Allison and
Assistant Secretary Earl Johnson of the State
Department and General Carter Magruder and
Colonel Stanton Babcock of the Defense Department, politely remarked how helpful the draft
would be and then methodically chipped away at
its six major points.

First, the Americans expressed reservations
regarding the call for a ten-year time limit.
They preferred a more flexible arrangement and
proposed the wording "until the security of
Japan can be effectively guaranteed by an alternative arrangement."[22] The American delegates
next turned to the Japanese provision on the
status of forces and asked for the right of un-
impeded passage in Japan. Iguchi and Nishimura
agreed, offering to stipulate it in their draft.
The Americans also asked Japan not to release
information on the location, equipment, or
strength of U.S. forces in Japan. Iguchi and
Nishimura again agreed. They observed that
these items were military secrets and proposed
that both countries might omit references to
them in the security treaty by leaving "the
details of the agreement" to a joint committee.
The Americans concurred.

Discussion on the remaining points revealed
U.S. discontent and wishes regarding Japan's
security policy. One item in the Japanese draft
contained an agreement to consult whenever both
countries recognized a threat to their sovereignty or independence. Even though they supported this provision, the Americans pressed
Japan for more concrete measures in implementing
it. They specifically called for the establishment of a national defense agency, alongside
the Foreign Ministry, so that Japan could have
institutions corresponding to the departments of
Defense and State. Allison, Johnson, and others
implied that Japan would benefit immeasurably
from better, more direct lines of communication
to Washington.

The American delegates then read the Japanese
recommendation on a joint committee and again
stressed the desirability of a defense agency.
They argued such an organization would permit
the Japanese government to have control over
security-related issues during joint committee
consultations with the American government. The
Japanese representatives, however, remained unpersuaded. In their view, a full-blown bureaucracy was unnecessary, for the government could
always use military specialists in talks with
the United States.

Discussion on the final two points went to the
crux of American desires. In its draft, the
Japanese government proposed to pay for the facilities and services which Japan would offer,
while America would cover the cost of troops
stationed in Japan. The American delegates informed Iguchi and Nishimura that the United
States would not be frugal in building Japan's
defense capabilities and would seek to lighten
Japanese responsibilities in this area.

Allison and Johnson then turned to the last
point in the Japanese draft, the provision for a
collective self-defense relationship based on

the United Nations Charter. Allison and Johnson
demanded a clearer indication of the means
whereby Japan would cooperate with America in
resisting an invasion.   Iguchi and Nishimura
replied that Japan's cooperation could include
its police force, industrial strength, and
transportation network.
     Allison and Johnson repeated the wish for a
more comprehensive statement.   They noted Japan's ability to maintain domestic order following increases in the National Police Reserves,
and emphasized U.S. interest in the next logical
step toward a ground force.   Iguchi and Nishimura, for their part, reiterated their earlier
position that Japan could make her considerable
productive strength available to America in lieu
of such a force, and ended the first session
with a request for the American security
proposal.[23]
     On February 2, the Japanese and American rep-
resentatives resumed their discussion. At that
time, U.S. delegates surprised Iguchi and Nishimura with a proposal to enumerate the rights and
privileges of U.S. forces in a security treaty.
Iguchi and Nishimura feared this proposal might
jeopardize the treaty's chances of early passage, stimulate domestic fears over a belliger-
ent Japan, and imply to the Japanese that the
Occupation would continue after independence
[Nishimura (a)].
     The Japanese representatives strongly protest-
ed, calling the provision a blow to Japanese
pride.   And the next day, they demanded its revision or deletion from the security treaty.[24]
The immediate concern of Iguchi and Nishimura
was not any one provision in the U.S. proposal,
but rather the feeling that talks were rapidly
deteriorating because of more fundamental differences over security policy.
     After the meeting on February 2, the two Jap-
anese met Yoshida to brief him on the negotia-

tions and to recommend a Tokyo rearmament concession. In order to avoid a breakdown in negotiations, Yoshida instructed Nishimura to draft
two items.[25]
The prime minister first told Nishimura to
produce a security treaty article that would
stress the desirability of a short accord and
entrust all defense responsibilities to a joint
committee. Yoshida felt this provision would
eliminate needless articles and, more important,
avoid direct reference to Japanese rearmament.
On February 3, Yoshida sent Allison "A Japan-
U.S. Cooperative Agreement on Mutual Security"
that included these items.
Yoshida then ordered Nishimura to draft a second document entitled "Initial Steps for Rearmament Planning":

Japan must begin a rearmament effort that will
coincide with the coming into effect of the
Peace Treaty and Japan-U.S. Mutual Security
Treaty. Toward that end, the Government of
Japan proposes to establish a 50,000-man national defense force consisting of land and
sea units. This force will exist separately
from the National Police Reserve and Maritime
Safety Forces. Furthermore, it will possess
weaponry superior to them and lay the basis
for a democratically reconstructed military in
Japan.
The Government of Japan also proposes to
establish a Peace Preservation Agency and a
Defense Planning Office. The Agency will correspond to the [American] Department of Defense, while the Office will correspond to a
general staff headquarters. Members of the
Defense Planning Office will include specialists in U.S.-U.K. military affairs. They will
participate in the joint committee to be established by the Japan-U.S. Mutual Security

Treaty and will welcome the advice of American
military officials.[26]

Two aspects of the Yoshida proposal deserving
attention are authorship and purpose. Nishimura
drafted the document after receiving detailed
instructions from the prime minister. In a pub-
lished interview, the Treaty Bureau director
speculated that Yoshida thought of the major
provisions following secret consultations with
his military advisers. A personal interview
with Tatsumi, however, seems to indicate that
the prime minister formulated the proposal
alone. During the interview, Tatsumi emphati-
cally denied knowledge of the plan [Tatsumi].
Ignorance by Yoshida's most trusted military
adviser and a self-imposed twenty-four-hour time
limit suggest that one man hurriedly snapped the
document together.
As for purpose, Yoshida evidently intended to
secure a peace settlement through a rearmament
plan that would least burden the Japanese economy. The core of this proposal was the 50,000-
man figure. The importance of a figure stemmed
from U.S. insistence for an indication of Japan's contribution. The importance of this figure flowed from its lack of significance in
strategic terms. In the opinion of Tatsumi, "A
50,000-man force was utter nonsense. It could
not have served any conceivable military purpose." General Headquarters seemed to agree.
In GHQ's estimate, defense of the home islands
required a force of 325,000--six and a half
times larger than what Yoshida proposed.
Tatsumi suggested that the basis may have been
financial: "A first-level military buildup
which Yoshida thought the nation could then
afford" [Tatsumi]. Because of his dual desires
to conclude peace and avoid rearmament, Yoshida
may have regarded a 50,000-man offer as some-

thing that could placate America without endan-
gering the economy.

Two days after receiving the proposal, Dulles
and his assistants met Iguchi and Nishimura.
Dulles spoke first, saying that the United
States was studying the "Japanese opinion on a
security treaty" and would offer an assessment
as soon as possible. Iguchi and Nishimura followed, raising Japanese concerns over Allied
property claims and industrial restrictions.

When they finished, Dulles handed them the
text and annex of the peace treaty in outline
form. He emphasized that these documents embodied the "Seven Principles of Peace" which would
serve as the basis of negotiations with the
Allies, and reiterated that America would work
for peace despite opposition from Communist and
non-Communist circles.[27]

The next day both sides met without Dulles in
attendance. Again, American representatives
pressed hard on the rearmament issue. Ostensibly responding to the Japanese security proposal,
they submitted a three-part statement that dis-
turbed Iguchi and Nishimura for what it omitted
rather than for what it contained.

Two of the three parts in fact supported Japanese wishes on a security treaty. One part
offered to list the legal privileges of U.S.
forces in an executive agreement, an accord not
requiring legislative approval. And a second
part agreed to stipulate Tokyo's right of individual and collective self-defense in a peace
treaty, as well as its ability to sign a collective security pact. Iguchi and Nishimura felt
the first provision would avoid a Diet debate
over military personnel, while the second provision would justify a separate security treaty
with America [Nishimura (a)].

The third part, an outline of the American
security proposal, evoked an unfavorable Japanese response. Except for a time limit, the U.S.

proposal did not refer to any of the major
points in the original Japanese draft of February 1. Particularly displeasing to Iguchi and
Nishimura was the legal basis--or nonbasis--of
the document. To their dismay, the American
document failed to recognize a collective security relationship based on the United Nations
Charter. The Japanese felt that a token reference to Article 51 in the title of the security
treaty was insufficient. They wanted something
more [Nishimura (b)].

The Americans retorted that a Charter-grounded
security relationship had not yet emerged. Until it did, U.S. troops would have to remain in
Japan and the security treaty would have to be
provisional.[28]

America's outright rejection of the Japanese
position shocked Iguchi and Nishimura. They
immediately asked for a reference, anywhere in
the preamble or the text, to a U.S.-Japan cooperative relationship that would protect Japan
according to provisions of the UN Charter. They
argued that Japan could contribute to its defense without a major military buildup. In
their opinion, Japan's labor pool and industrial
capacity would assist the American defense of
Japan. An even more important contribution,
they stressed, would be permission to maintain
bases throughout Japan. Iguchi and Nishimura
finally contended a collective self-defense relationship to be appropriate because the interests of both countries would be served by a
security arrangement. Thus, the elements of
benefit and sacrifice would not be unfairly
weighted but, rather, equitably balanced between
the two sides.

These arguments failed to impress the Americans. Allison, Johnson, and Magruder said that
Japan lacked the means to ensure her own defense
and further stressed that the Vandenberg Resolu-
tion (1948) permitted U.S. participation in col-

lective security arrangements affecting U.S.
security interests and adhering to self-help and
mutual assistance. Because the arrangement with
Japan fell short of the latter requirements,
America would have to refrain from signing a
mutual defense pact with Japan. For Iguchi and
Nishimura the message was implicit but obvious:
only a more substantial rearmament proposal
could satisfy American officials and secure the
type of treaty they wanted.

Yoshida was not prepared to up his offer, however. In meetings with MacArthur on February 6
and Dulles on February 7, the prime minister
showed no intention of bowing to American pressure. During his talks with MacArthur, Yoshida
stressed differences with Dulles over the Ryuku
and Bonin islands. He "apologized" for the disagreement over the territories issue, and said
he had simply tried to convey the wishes of the
Japanese people, to whom he was politically responsible. Yoshida then stated his willingness
to accept the articles on territories in their
final form.

The prime minister next displayed sensitivity
on the rearmament issue, when he asked the
United States to delete any peace treaty article
characterizing the National Police Reserve as a
military force. MacArthur agreed.

Yoshida concluded his remarks by referring to
his limited rearmament plan and stressing his
desire to build a democratic army of 50,000 men
and a general staff headquarters based on a
U.S.-U.K. model. In his opinion, the German-
style military of Meiji was a mistake that must
not be repeated. MacArthur accepted Yoshida's
plan with some reluctance. The general then
warned that advances had occurred in weapons
technology; therefore, Japan's military class,
which had been out of touch for five years,
would be useless to the prime minister.

The next day Yoshida met Dulles and Johnson.
He first gave Dulles a letter on the fisheries

issue. Then turning to his proposal, Yoshida asked Dulles to omit any reference in the peace treaty to Japan's willingness to rearm. Dulles said he understood the prime minister's position, and promised to stipulate that America would put no constraints on a Japanese military buildup.

Yoshida repeated the wish for a new armed force whose organization and individuals would look to America for guidance, and then stressed his expectation of U.S. assistance in building such a force. Japan responded with support for the prime minister's statement and pledged to forward it to Washington.

The following day Iguchi and Allison met to initial tentative acceptance of the peace treaty, security treaty, and administrative agreement. The decisions to sign, which were made despite both Japanese and American dissatisfaction over the course of negotiations, revealed the disparity in bargaining strength.

For Yoshida, Iguchi, and Nishimura the decision to agree underscored Japanese weakness. In their view, they were forced to accept an unequal security treaty and offer a limited rearmament plan in order to secure a peace settlement for Japan. No one was pleased.[29]

For Dulles, Allison, Johnson, and Magruder the decision to initial highlighted American strength. Except for a separate executive agreement, the major deference to Japanese wishes was acceptance of the 50,000-man proposal. According to one official, U.S. representatives were "not thrilled" about the offer. In their view, it was "better than nothing but inadequate."[30] Nevertheless, they accepted.

The American officials felt a 50,000-man figure to be the last offer that Yoshida would make. They also knew it was the only offer that he had ever made. After great difficulty with Yoshida over the military question, State and Defense Department planners had finally secured

his promise to rearm. Having won this concession, the Americans evidently consoled themselves with the thought of accepting the promise
but not the figure. Several years later, as
ambassador to Japan, Allison felt the United
States could persuade Japan to rearm rapidly.
Continued recalcitrance, however, would eventually cause him to accept a low Japanese profile
on defense [Allison].

In February 1951, Allison, Dulles, and others
apparently decided to postpone pressure for
greater buildup. In their view, the conclusion
of the peace and security treaties would have to
come first. But they could afford to wait. After all, the advantages seemed to be on their
side.

THE PRICE OF RATIFICATION, 1951-1952

The China Requirement

Sino-Japanese relations and American bases were strange policy bedfellows. Substantively speaking, they had nothing to do with each other. Procedurally speaking, however, they had much in common. After the San Francisco Peace Conference (September 1951), the United States Senate threatened to withhold treaty ratification unless the president obtained Japanese concessions on both issues [Allison]. Certainly, Tokyo-Washington differences on China and bases had existed before the conference. But they had been papered over in a set of understandings worked out between the two sides. From October 1951 that would no longer be possible.

In the case of Communist China, Japanese leaders pursued policies favoring diplomatic contact with Peking. Prime Minister Yoshida, the principal architect of China policy in 1951 and 1952, actively supported a reestablishment of relations with the Mainland [Fujisaki; Nishimura (b)]. And American opposition notwithstanding, he constructed proposals more closely akin to major power detente of the 1970s than to cold war containment of the 1950s.

This early orientation toward Peking evolved from Yoshida's prewar years in China and his reading of events throughout Asia. During the 1920s Yoshida served in several diplomatic posts on the Mainland. Tours of duty in Tientsin (1922-1925) and Mukden (1928) became the prism through which he perceived the People's Republic. From his experiences, Yoshida felt the

several millennia of contact and cultural affin-
ity meant that Japan must continue a special relationship with the Mainland [Fujisaki; Taka-
hashi]. He realized, of course, that success or
failure depended upon the Communist leadership's
response. Its recent actions, including the
signing of the Sino-Soviet Friendship Treaty and
involvement in the Korean War, realistically
prohibited the development of Japanese-Chinese
ties in the near future. What Yoshida therefore
wanted was some diplomatic posture that would
enable Tokyo to establish relations with Peking
in the distant future [Ibid.].
    Moreover, Yoshida judged that the government
of Chiang Kai-shek was politically dead. He
estimated that the Nationalists could never re-
take the Mainland. And though he felt grateful
to Chiang for the early repatriation of Japanese
prisoners of war, Yoshida feared that any commitment to Taiwan would be at the expense of
Japan's future ties to the Mainland. In his
judgment, the People's Republic would refuse to
establish relations with a Japanese government
that had legally supported the Nationalist
regime [Ibid.].
    Finally, Yoshida dismissed the existence of a
strategic threat arising from the Sino-Soviet
alliance. In an April 8, 1950, conversation
with diplomatic counselor Cloyce Huston, Yoshida
mentioned his belief that "China would never become a slave of the Kremlin. Referring to cen-
turies of Chinese history, the character of the
Chinese people, their consistent successes in
the past in thwarting efforts at domination or
absorption, and their superriority to the Rus-
sians in intelligence, cleverness, and political
astuteness, he declared that he had every confidence in the outcome."[1] Yoshida also told his
advisers in the Foreign Ministry that these
traits of Chinese ethnocentrism and superiority
would inevitably lead to a clash or rivalry with

Soviet leaders [Fujisaki]. As he mentioned to
one friend, the Chinese Communists were Chinese
first and Communists second [Hagiwara].

Before the San Francisco Peace Conference,
John Foster Dulles and Prime Minister Yoshida
averted conflict over China policy by a series
of secret agreements. On April 11, 1951, President Truman publicly relieved General MacArthur
of all his commands. And one week later, the
president sent Dulles to Tokyo to assure the
Japanese that MacArthur's dismissal would not
sidetrack the peace settlement. When Dulles and
General Matthew Ridgway (the new SCAP) met Yoshida on April 18, they reiterated Truman's determination to conclude a treaty with Japan.

After that meeting Dulles made a second call
on the prime minister. The U.S. representative
first mentioned the continuation of the harsh
Philippine attitude on Japanese reparations. He
then asked Yoshida to consider some form of production reparations that might appease Philippine leaders and induce their support of a liberal Japanesee accord [Nishimura (b)]. Dulles
also told the prime minister about the formation
of a trilateral Australian-New Zealand-United
States security pact, whose function would be to
guard against a revival of Japanese militarism
in the future.[2]

Dulles then informed Yoshida that he had received the British draft of a Japanese peace
treaty in early April. He referred to one provision that troubled him: the call for Communist Chinese participation at a Japanese treaty
conference. In his opinion, the U.S. Senate
would staunchly oppose a peace settlement that
included the P.R.C. Dulles thereupon informed
Yoshida of his intention to visit London to re-
concile U.S.-U.K. differences over this matter.
Meanwhile, he wanted some assurance regarding
Japan's support for the American position on
China. Yoshida agreed [Nishimura (b)].

During the meeting on April 23, Dulles offered
the prime minister several procedures whereby
the two governments would adopt consistent policies vis-a-vis the P.R.C. The procedure Yoshida
selected was an oral pledge not to sign a separate peace treaty with the Mainland.[3] Two months
later, on June 19, Dulles secured British agreement to a formula that excluded the P.R.C. and
R.O.C. from a conference, while permitting Japan
to sign a peace treaty with the China of her
choice. While in London, Dulles suffered a con-
venient memory lapse about the Yoshida pledge
[Allison]. He obtained British support of a
formula that was less a compromise and more a
concession to American wishes on China.
    Dulles and Yoshida thus sidestepped the China
representation issue by the prime minister's
pledge and the U.S.-U.K. "compromise" formula
that offered everything to everybody. The Senate and State Department could assure themselves
that Yoshida would not legally commit Japan to
the People's Republic. The British could pre-
sume that the absence of two Chinas would not
necessarily preclude the development of P.R.C.-
Japan relations. And Prime Minister Yoshida
could feel that he had not openly embraced Taipei to the abandonment of Peking.
    During the San Francisco Peace Conference,
Japanese and American officials maintained this
delicate balance of understandings on China. On
September 3, John Foster Dulles and Secretary of
State Dean Acheson paid a courtesy call on the
visiting Japanese prime minister. After a brief
discussion on reparations, Yoshida asked Acheson
whether he would demand an immediate decision
regarding Japan's choice of diplomatic partner.
The prime minister knew the kind of impact such
an announcement would have upon the conference,
and therefore seemed to be asking a question
whose answer was predetermined. The Secretary's
response did not disappoint him. Acheson re-

plied that Japan should not announce any decision on China, for the supporters of the regime
not selected would be alienated from the
conference.

Dulles then pressured Yoshida for the decision
that the prime minister would eventually have to
make. First mentioning that the choice of
Chinas was a matter for the Japanese government,
he reminded Yoshida of his earlier "personal
message" in support of Taiwan. Dulles also
warned that relations with the P.R.C. could lead
to Senate rejection of the peace and security
treaties, and stressed that Tokyo must maintain
its close economic and personal ties with
Taipei.

Eight weeks later the China issue quickly
surfaced in a diplomatic explosion. The spark
was provided by the prime minister. On October
29 Yoshida testified before the Special Diet
Committee considering peace and security treaty
ratification. In response to questions over his
China policy, Yoshida entered into a discussion
about overseas offices. In his view, such offices might serve two diplomatic functions: the
development of trade and commerce with another
nation, and the protection of Japanese nationals
abroad. The prime minister then reiterated his
interest in opening several overseas offices to
facilitate the growth of economic ties around
the world.

Yoshida next turned to Taiwan and noted the
existence of a Japanese overseas office there.
But he cautioned that it was not a political act
recognizing the R.O.C. as the government of
China. In addition, Yoshida inidcated his
willingness to establish a similar overseas
office in Shanghai, if the P.R.C. were to request one. In conclusion, Yoshida said the
P.R.C. would be welcome to open an office in
Japan, as long as the purpose were trade and not
propaganda- or conflict-related.[5]

The Washington reaction was immediate. Yoshida's veiled reference to trade with Peking distressed John Sparkman, Alexander Smith, and other influential senators. In their view, the prime minister seemed to be not only leaning publicly toward relations with Peking but also reneging on his earlier pledge not to sign a separate treaty with the Communist regime. The senators consequently demanded that Dulles visit Tokyo a fourth time to obtain Yoshida's written promise not to have relations with the P.R.C. [Allison].

The obvious question that arises concerns the reason for the prime minister's statement. Presumably any statement about economic ties with Peking would displease Senate supporters of Taipei. Why then did Yoshida make such an announcement in a public forum?

Treaty Bureau director Kumao Nishimura offered an answer emphasizing the prime minister's personality. In his opinion, Yoshida should have calculated that an outburst over China might provoke an unfavorable American response. The exercise of greater self-control could have avoided a diplomatic rift with America and permitted the pursuit of low-level contact with Peking. Despite the foolhardiness of Yoshida's remarks, though, they were not surprising to Nishimura. According to the Treaty Bureau director, the Japanese prime minister often acted impulsively and unpredictably; he would sometimes do things for no rational reason. Nishimura suggested the China statement may have been an example of such behavior and added, "Yoshida must accept some responsibility for the unfortunate result that followed" [Nishimura (b)].

By "unfortunate result" Nishimura meant the conclusion of the peace treaty with Taiwan that, during negotiations with Dulles (December 1951) and the Republic of China (February 1952), Yoshida had tried to avoid.

In preparation for Dulles' arrival in December, Japanese planners focused on two separate
signals emanating from the U.S. government. The
first signal consisted of press stories indicating the importance of China as one of several
issues to be discussed. News reports of November 20, 22, and 29 not only mentioned possible
talks over Japanese rearmament but also stressed
the unhappiness of Dulles, Sparkman, and Smith
over Japan's wish to establish relations with
Mainland China. The reports, moreover, cited
the intention of the three men to work for peace
treaty ratification while in Japan.
   This implicit linkage between China policy and
treaty passage stirred uneasy feelings within
the Japanese Treaty Bureau. Nevertheless, bureau members took some comfort in the upcoming
opportunity to present Japanese wishes over the
administrative agreement, reparations policy,
and other key issues.[6]
   During a press conference in Tokyo on December
11, the three U.S. representatives again mentioned their interest on the China issue. Although steadfastly affirming their neutrality
regarding Japan's choice of diplomatic partner,
they indicated their "willingness" to respond to
any inquiries from Japan on this matter. The
Americans also stressed the need for a first-
step buildup that would enable Japan to deter an
indirect invasion of the country.[7]
   The second signal to Japanese leaders came in
the form of a message from Dulles. On December
12, Dulles met Vice Minister of Foreign Affairs
Sadao Iguchi. Dulles referred to the great influence of powerful Democrats and Republicans on
the China issue, and pressed for Japanese recognition of the Nationalist government. Dulles
then emphasized that the Yoshida government
would not only have to enter into friendly relations with the R.O.C. but would also have to
give proof of its intention to do so.[8]

Yoshida's October 29 statement and his San
Francisco meeting with Acheson evidently impressed Dulles with the prime minister's reluctance to agree to ties with Taipei. To induce a
Yoshida promise to recognize the Nationalist
government, Dulles offered Iguchi a concession
of sorts. While advocating the desirability of
Japan-R.O.C. ties, Dulles reiterated that the
extent of relations could be limited to the area
actually under Nationalist control. Thus, the
U.S. representative effectively proposed to exclude the Mainland from any formal arrangement
between Tokyo and Taipei.[9]
    After hearing Dulles' message, Yoshida in-
structed Treaty Bureau director Kumao Nishimura
to draft a formal proposal for presentation to
the American representative. The goal of this
document was to minimize the degree of Japan's
legal commitment to Taiwan. Yoshida felt that a
formal peace treaty with the R.O.C. would stif-
fen the P.R.C.'s attitude against Japan, and
thereby prevent the development of a Japan-
P.R.C. diplomatic line. In Yoshida's view, a
peace treaty with Chiang Kai-shek held a "zero-
minus" relationship for Japan and the two Chinas: nothing to gain with Taipei and everything
to lose with Peking.
    The proposal contained three sections that
sought to avoid the peace treaty that Yoshida
feared. The first section mentioned Japanese
aspirations for peace and security in the Far
East. It also stressed that confusion over
China representation had prevented Japan from
complying with Article 26 of the San Francisco
Peace Settlement, which provided for peace
treaties with nonsignatory powers [Nishimura
(b)].[10]
    To support this point, Yoshida was prepared to
argue that Japan could not sign a peace treaty
until America and Great Britain had settled
their differences over China representation

[Nishimura (b)]. The prime minister knew about
U.S.-U.K. disagreement over this issue and about
speculation regarding a Churchill visit to Washington in the near future. Yoshida evidently
wished to benefit from any drag British opposition might exert on U.S. policy toward China.
By linking Japan's choice of diplomatic partner
to U.S.-U.K. agreement on China policy, he apparently intended to halt a Dulles-induced rush
toward peace with Taiwan.

The second section of the proposal incorporated Dulles' offer to Iguchi of a jurisdictional
limitation in Japan-R.O.C. relations. It mentioned that any arrangement on normalization
with Taiwan would relate only to the area under
de facto control of that government.

Besides geographic restrictions and time
delay, the Yoshida proposal called for a third
delimiting device. In accordance with Article
21 of the San Francisco Peace Settlement, Yoshida proposed to normalize relations with Taiwan
by the exchange of special envoys, the conclusion of treaties of commerce and navigation, and
the like [Nishimura (a)]. Japan and Nationalist
China would thus achieve normalization through a
series of economic arrangements rather than a
peace treaty. Yoshida hoped this provision
would satisfy Dulles' demand for a commitment to
Taiwan while averting a full-scale legal relationship that might alienate the Mainland.

On the afternoon of December 13 both leaders
met again. Dulles strongly argued that Japan
should enter into a treaty with the Republic of
China. The agreement would relate only to the
area under actual control, and "relations with
the area over which Taiwan [had] no de facto
control would be left for later determination."[11]

Yoshida tried to counter Dulles. He offered
his proposal on China and a series of oral arguments supporting Japan-P.R.C. contact. Yoshida

argued that the China issue could not be settled
by force. He also emphasized that political,
economic, and cultural links between China and
the free world should be expanded instead of re-
duced; otherwise, the people under Communist
rule could never realize the attractiveness of
freedom nor perceive the desirability of joining
the free world [Nishimura (b)].[12]
Yoshida then emphasized that Japan, unlike
America, had always been a neighbor of China.
Cultural similarities with China had existed far
longer than those between the United States and
the United Kingdom. The prime minister further
mentioned his hope that America allow Japan to
expand contacts with the P.R.C., and he asked
for Dulles' confidence that Japan would not join
the Mainland [Nishimura (b)]. At one point, he
almost repeated an earlier remark to Dean Rusk
that such a role could be Japan's "contribution
. . . in the post-treaty period" [Rusk].[13]
     The prime minister concluded by stressing that
the present situation over China had arisen
from a breakdown in Allied cooperation. Yoshida
argued only U.S.-U.K. consensus on China policy
could resolve this issue. And he added that the
beginning toward consensus might occur during
Churchill's forthcoming visit to America.[14]
     Dulles apparently dismissed Yoshida's calls
for contact between Japan and Communist China as
a political fantasy. He mentioned his disap-
pointment over the Yoshida proposal, which he
felt did not go far enough.[15] In Dulles' view,
anything short of a Japanese-Nationalist Chinese
peace treaty was unacceptable. To highlight
Japan's adoption of a pro-Taiwan position, Dulles spent the morning of December 17 drafting a
letter that Yoshida should send him. According
to William Sebald, the letter was a short statement of "Japanese policy towards the Chinese Nationalist Government and the Communist Chinese
Government."[16]

When the two leaders met again on December 18,
Dulles began with a pointed reference to Yoshida's speech of October 29. He stated the debate
over China policy in the Diet had fired Senate
doubts about Japanese reliability. To alleviate
the concerns of powerful R.O.C. backers, the
Japanese government would have to promise publicly to sign a peace treaty with Taiwan. Dulles stressed that such a pledge would illustrate
U.S.-Japan cooperation on China, and further
said that the timing of release could be discussed by the two governments [Nishimura (a)].[17]
He then handed to Yoshida a draft of the letter that Yoshida should sign and send him. In
addition, he pointed to one paragraph which
might overcome Yoshida's demand for delay until
U.S.-U.K. agreement on China policy--namely,
Japan's prerogative to recognize the R.O.C. as a
government of China and not as the government of
China. Dulles hoped this basis of recognition
would mollify Yoshida by removing the Communist
China question from a Tokyo-Taipei peace accord.
Thus, the Japanese prime minister could move
toward the Nationalist government without feeling publicly forced to renounce the Communist
regime.
Dulles also informed Yoshida of his lack of
interest in the contents of the accord. In his
opinion, Japan could make any series of demands
during negotiations with Taiwan. He reiterated,
however, that the title of the document would
have to be a "bilateral peace treaty."
The difficulty for Yoshida was the narrrowing
of response to a clear yes or no. Because of
Senate unhappiness over Yoshida's speech of
October 29, Dulles had forced the prime minister
to choose between agreeing or disagreeing to a
bilateral peace settlement with Taiwan. Even
though agreement would presumably ensure ratification of the San Francisco treaties, it would
end Yoshida's dream of relations with Communist

China. Conversely, disagreement would permit
the development of ties with the Mainland, but
at the cost of perpetuating Japan's nonindepen-
dent status.

The prime minister judged the two choices to
be unacceptable, for he was strongly committed
to a diplomatic relationship with Peking and a
peace settlement for Japan. In an interview,
Nishimura explained, "Prime Minister Yoshida was
for the most part a political realist. He calculated what Japan's objective interests were
and what policies would protect them. But on
China policy, he was clearly an idealist, perhaps even a visionary. . . . He simply could not
stand the thought of a U.S. wall separating
Japan from the Mainland" [Nishimura (b)].

Caught in a policy dilemma, the prime minister
tried to forge an alternative path leading to
the P.R.C. On December 18, Yoshida agreed to
sign the Yoshida letter and, the next day, suggested strengthening it with a reference to the
Sino-Soviet Friendship Treaty [Nishimura (b)].[18]
In addition, he pledged to conclude a bilateral
treaty with Taiwan. Pleased with Yoshida's ap-
parent concession, Dulles left for Washington on
December 20.

Dulles evidently failed to grasp the precise
nature of Yoshida's response. The prime minister agreed to conclude a bilateral treaty with
Taiwan, not a bilateral peace treaty. The
intended difference was enormous. By bilateral
treaty, Yoshida meant an economic agreement that
would fall short of a peace settlement but still
normalize relations with Taiwan. He apparently
hoped this promise would ease U.S. pressure on
China policy by giving Dulles the false impression of Japanese agreement to peace with Taiwan
[Nishimura (b)].

At the time, Yoshida evidently intended to
secure a normalization treaty with Taiwan and
later feign a misunderstanding with Dulles. The

prime minister may have felt the momentum toward
a Japanese peace treaty and the importance of
coming administrative agreement talks would
force America to overlook Japan's "inadvertent"
misstep, which could be corrected after Senate
ratification.

For the moment, Yoshida's deception apparently
worked. After returning to Washington, Dulles
informed the British government of Japan's desire to have a bilateral peace settlement with
the Republic of China. During the visit of Foreign Minister Anthony Eden to Washington in December 1951, Dulles sent an explanation of the
Yoshida letter to that government. He assumed
the contents would be transmitted to the visiting British foreign minister [Rusk]. For still
unexplained reasons, they were not.

Upon returning to London, Eden became aware of
the letter for the first time through a series
of press reports. The release of the document
stimulated a Parliamentary assault that took the
Churchill Cabinet completely by surprise. Although opposition criticism did not prove fatal,
news reports of the letter and the imperfect
flow of information within the British government combined to produce a minor crisis for
America's closest ally [Allison].[19]

The release of the Yoshida letter evidently
led to difficulties for the Japanese government
as well. Following its publication on January
16, 1952, the Republic of China openly pressed
for the start of negotiations in Taipei over a
peace accord. Yoshida responded with the decision to send a delegation including Torao Ushiroku and Shiroshichi Kimura. Ushiroku had served as a junior-level diplomat in China during
the war (1942-1945) and in 1952 occupied the
China desk in the Foreign Ministry. Kimura had
prewar diplomatic experience, but his greatest
asset was his blood relationship to Yoshida.
The prime minister felt Chinese negotiators

would react favorably to his demonstration of personal interest in the talks [Ushiroku].

After Yoshida's decision to send a diplomatic team to Taiwan, Treaty Bureau director Nishimura "patched together" a document that could be negotiated quickly with the Republic of China. According to Ushiroku, the draft took less than a week to put together. It focused narrowly on economic relations and consisted of twelve or thirteen clauses, including provisions for negotiating claims and normalizing trade relations.

The legal basis of the document was not Article 26 of the San Francisco Peace Treaty, which provided for conclusion of peace settlements with nonsignatory powers, but rather Article 21, which called for establishment of economic relations between Japan and Taiwan. To avoid protracted negotiations over substance, the Japanese draft began with a basket clause: "Unless otherwise provided in the treaty, the relevant provisions of the San Francisco Peace Treaty apply." This clause would allow Japanese representatives to minimize the importance of calling the accord a peace settlement, with the argument that it duplicated the San Francisco agreement. In the Treaty Bureau view, the R.O.C. would immediately recognize the reasonableness of the Japanese position and, after two weeks of technical adjustments, would acquiesce to it.

Unfortunately for the Japanese representatives, their Chinese counterparts were not so accommodating. During the first day of talks, R.O.C. representatives refused to begin negotiations until Japan agreed to call the document a peace settlement. After four or five days of standstill, both sides drafted a secret memo and reached an understanding. According to the memo and the understanding, Japan tentatively agreed to call the accord a peace settlement. That title would remain if the contents of the negotiated final product approximated a peace set-

tlement. Should the contents differ, the final
document would be called something else. Thus,
an agreement consisting entirely of economic
provisions would presumably be entitled a trade
or normalization accord.

Japanese delegates gave their support to this
understanding without prior consultation with
the Foreign Ministry; they asked Tokyo for approval only after tentatively committing Japan
to peace with Taiwan [Ushiroku]. Their decision
to support a peace accord, even a tentative one,
transgressed the basic principle of Yoshida's
China policy. When the prime minister heard of
the understanding on peace, he became furious at
his cousin, chief delegate Kimura. At that time
Yoshida felt that a so-called tentative agreement amounted to a formal Japanese concession to
Taiwan [Nishimura (b)].

His negotiating team apparently made this decision because of an incomplete reading of Yoshida's intentions. The delegates were aware of
the prime minister's desire to minimize Japan's
legal commitment to Taiwan; they seemed to be
confused, however, over the appropriate political means at their disposal. In their view, the
best way to minimize an international commitment
to Taiwan would be to delimit Taipei's authority
to the area under de facto control. In Kimura
and Ushiroku's view, the title was a matter of
secondary importance. Despite their vague
awareness of Yoshida's wish to avoid a bilateral
peace treaty with Taiwan, the delegates did not
have a clear idea of a formal title before leaving Japan. Under the terms of the Yoshida letter, they judged that the prime minister had already committed Japan to a bilateral peace
treaty with Taiwan sometime in the future
[Ushiroku].

Two explanations may be offered for his delegates' ignorance of Yoshida's strong opposition
to a peace settlement. The prime minister may

have simply failed to give clear instructions
concerning the nonnegotiable nature of the
title. As mentioned earlier, Foreign Ministry
officials hastily prepared for talks with the
R.O.C. Under those circumstances, a misunderstanding on negotiating policy could have easily
occurred.

Alternatively, the prime minister may have
chosen not to inform the delegates fully of his
wishes on China policy. Yoshida evidently refrained from telling the representatives of his
deception of Dulles. He apparently decided to
reduce the chance of news leak and political
fallout by keeping a tight lid on information.
Although prepared to inform the delegates of his
general opposition to peace, the prime minister
evidently decided against risking a diplomatic
incident by passing along information that would
underscore his commitment to a non-peace
agreement.

Whether because of misunderstanding or ignorance, the Japanese deleegates made a second concession to the Nationalist side. Because of
R.O.C. intransigence and the perceived need to
finalize an accord, the delegates agreed to extend the document with Taiwan beyond the area
under de facto control to an area of potential
control (i.e., "territories which are now, or
which may hereafter be, under control").

In Kimura and Ushiroku's view, this phrase
unfortunately implied a Japanese pledge to recognize Chiang's claims over the Mainland [Ushi-
roku]. Had it been omitted, the treaty would
not have referred indirectly to the P.R.C., with
provisions on Japan's indemnities dating from
the Boxer Rebellion.

To avoid domestic difficulties, Japanese officials depicted the treaty differently before the
Diet. During appearances there, Foreign Minister Katsuo Okazaki and others solemnly swore
that the treaty with Taiwan did not extend to

the Mainland.[20]   Reality, however, was different. Because of misjudgment and uncertainty,
the prime minister found himself burdened with a
political albatross of sorts--namely, a bilateral peace treaty that vaguely recognized Taiwan's pretensions to be the government of China.
It was indeed a most curious ending to a most
curious succession of events.

The Administrative Agreement

On February 2, 1951, Sadao Iguchi and Kumao
Nishimura first learned of American plans to
stipulate U.S. military rights and privileges in
a security treaty. At that time they strongly
protested, warning that an enumeration of legal
exemptions could suggest American extraterri-
toriality in post-treaty Japan.
Four days later, U.S. delegates offered to
relegate these provisions to an executive agreement not requiring legislative approval. John
Allison and others apparently felt a procedural
repackaging could ease Diet pressure on Yoshida
while protecting base personnel in Japan. Despite objections to several items, Iguchi and
Nishimura accepted. In their judgment, conclusion of the peace treaty had priority over further wrangling on a subsidiary accord.
In June 1951, following publication of the
NATO Status of Forces Agreement, Japanese planners took a second look at the administrative
agreement. From the Japanese viewpoint, SOFA
signaled a major shift in U.S. policy that could
be used to Tokyo's advantage. Most important,
it applied a new legal principle in relations
between host country and visiting military
force. Until SOFA, international precedent
seemed to discriminate in favor of the latter,
since visiting forces had exacted legal rights
as victor after war or as mother country fol-

lowing grants of independence to colonial areas.
But SOFA was different. Japanese leaders
believed that it established a collective security relationship based on equality: the collective security relationship stemmed from provisions of the United Nations Charter, while
equality derived from limited host state control
over the American military presence.[21]
SOFA gave Tokyo officials another reason for
elation. Yoshida and others knew about ongoing
negotiations between the United States and the
North Atlantic Allies on the status of American
forces in those countries. Although unaware of
specifics, they felt that Japan should wait for
the end of those talks rather than demand a re-
opening of negotiations with the United
States.[22] Yoshida and the Treaty Bureau judged
that Japan's strength lay in U.S. vulnerability
to criticism of offering a generous SOFA to Western Europe but not to Japan.
Using the detailed provisions of the NATO
accord as a model, the Treaty Bureau produced a
new, eighteen-article version of an administrative agreement which Yoshida would later approve
in revised form.
In early 1952 Foreign Minister Katsuo Okazaki
assisted Yoshida and Nishimura in the planning
and negotiations on an accord. Okazaki, who had
gained the confidence of the prime minister
while serving as Central Liaison Office director
during Yoshida's first Cabinet and chief secretary during his second, shared the concerns of
his prime minister and the Treaty Bureau director on a base accord. All three men abhored the
exemptions and privileges enjoyed by Occupation
forces in Japan, and they staunchly opposed a
continuation of them after independence. Okazaki, Yoshida, and Nishimura also worried that
opposition attempts to portray Japan as a colony
of imperial America would erode U.S. support for
an ungrateful ally [Nakajima]. To alleviate

both concerns, they adopted a policy of establishing administrative control over U.S. forces
in Japan. The purpose would be to punctuate
political equality and diplomatic partnership in
relations with America [Nishimura (a)].

   In Washington, planning started under a different set of objectives and priorities. Several months after the San Francisco Peace Conference, President Truman told the Senate that he
favored quick passage of the peace and security
treaties. Failure, he feared, would drag the
treaties into an election year debate and "increase the difficulty of getting the requisite
Senate vote."[23]

   The Joint Chiefs of Staff, however, opposed
the president's plans. In their view, "Senate
ratification of the U.S.-Japan Security Treaty
should not be completed until Japanese acceptance of the Administrative Agreement were obtained."[24] Delay, as Dulles suggested, would
permit the Joint Chiefs to "preserve the command
relationship" in Japan and "bargain for position
under the Security Treaty and Administrative
Agreement."[25] The Senate supported Pentagon
wishes for strict U.S. military control in Japan, and therefore agreed to hold up ratification
until the end of administrative agreement talks.

   In response to Senate and Pentagon demands,
President Truman instructed Dean Rusk, then assistant secretary of state for Far Eastern
affairs, to negotiate an executive accord with
Japan. In January 1952 Truman summoned Rusk to
the White House. During that meeting, Rusk explained State Department position papers on U.S.
legal rights in Japan. The President listened
patiently for some time and then confessed that
he had understood very little of what Rusk had
said. Truman thereupon mentioned his desire for
an agreement that would approximate the NATO
model and discriminate neither in favor of nor
against the Japanese [Rusk].

Because of Senate stall, the President evidently wanted an innocuous document which would
not create further difficulties with the Congress or the military. He was therefore more
concerned with securing military rights for his
American audience than with helping Japanese
leaders fight off domestic critics.

The negotiations that ensued spanned a four-
week period between January 29 and February 28,
1952. Despite numerous meetings between the
technical staffs, all the major points were
handled in the few fiery sessions between
Okazaki and Rusk. The issues inflaming those
talks narrowed down to a list of three. Of
them, "united command" proved to be the most
difficult for the Japanese. Nevertheless, it
was the only area in which they achieved a major
degree of success.

In its original and revised administrative
agreement (February and December 1951), America
provided for Japanese-U.S. defense cooperation
"in the event of hostilities or immediately
threatened hostilities in the Japan area."
Article 4 of the original text, for example,
placed the "National Police Reserve, and all
other Japanese organizations having military
potential . . . , under the unified command of a
supreme commander" who would be empowered "to
use such areas, installations and facilities in
the Japan area and to make such strategic and
tactical dispositions of military forces as he
may deem necessary."[26]

Yoshida understood America's inclination to
apply the NATO concepts of combined military
forces and U.S. supreme command to the case of
Japan. But for domestic political reasons he
would have to oppose united command. Yoshida
himself did not worry about American efforts to
use the concept as a pretext for introducing
Japanese troops into Korea. What concerned him,
though, were opposition attempts to draw this
and more unfavorable interpretations from it.

The prime minister consequently told Okazaki
that united command must be deleted. His position was nonnegotiable [Nishimura (a)].[27]
In encounters with Rusk, Okazaki presented a
matrix of legal, strategic, and political objections to united command. He of course repeated
the policy line concerning constitutional prohibitions on the use of force. But in addition,
Okazaki tried something new.

As mentioned earlier, U.S. officials in February 1951 had withheld support for a collective
self-defense arrangement in order to press Yoshida for a larger rearmament pledge. The prime
minister, however, refused to yield. As a result, American representatives refrained from
elevating the status of the treaty or offering a
clear commitment to defend Japan.

Okazaki attempted to use this point to his advantage. He contended that it was contradictory
for the United States to offer a defense commitment in an accord not subject to Diet inspection, while evading it in a security treaty requiring legislative approval. The Diet's right
to review international agreements suggested
that a reversal was in order. The United
States, he argued, should include a collective
self-defense commitment in the security treaty
and delete united command from the executive
accord [Nishimura (a)].

Accompanied later by Nishimura, Okazaki also
made a strategic argument emphasizing the point-
lessness of united command. In the view of Okazaki and Nishimura, a Soviet attack appeared to
be unlikely after conclusion of the U.S.-Japan
security treaty. But they added that the Japanese government would gladly place National Police Reserves and other paramilitary forces under
U.S. command in the event of a Communist attack.

Okazaki next explained the political damage
that united command would inflict on both countries:

The effective date of the Peace Treaty was
rapidly approaching, and I felt neither country would benefit from a breakdown in negotiations after having resolved the other major
issues in an administrative agreement.
    I explained to Rusk the feelings of the
Japanese people and the general situation in
U.S.-Japan relations. I also emphasized the
harsh Japanese war experience and the damage
that would be done to bilateral ties if the
Japanese government . appeared to be a mere
agent for U.S. military interests. From this
larger perspective, I argued that the U.S.
should accede to Japanese wishes on united
command.[28]

Though Rusk countered Okazaki's arguments, he
seemed to support the Japanese position. During
one session, the U.S. representative told Okazaki that America understood Tokyo's concerns.
He also said that the United States did not wish
to embarrass the Yoshida government, and would
therefore accept its suggestion to stipulate an
"agreement to consult" in event of attack.[29]
    Several factors weighed heavily in Rusk's de-
cision to concede. He firmly believed both
sides could not "legislate" an agreement cover-
ing a situation which had not yet occurred, and
further felt a provision on united command would
be ineffective unless both governments were willing to support it when an attack did occur
[Rusk]. The U.S. negotiator also judged that
the United States had sufficient firepower in
Japan to forestall a Soviet advance southward.
In his estimate, the chances of a military
strike that would trigger united command seemed
to be small.
    Rusk moreover shared Okazaki's concern over
domestic opposition to united command and its
long-term impact on U.S.-Japan relations. Rusk
attached great importance to Japanese public

opinion.   In his view, a key ingredient of security was public willingness to support a collective defense policy.   For this reason Rusk
had advocated the reversion of the Ryukus to
Japan in 1950, believing the consolidation of
security relations with Japan to be more important than a chain of islands which the Soviets
could destroy with one atomic bomb.   In his
opinion, it would not pay to come out of World
War II with an irredentist, anti-American Japan
     Finally, Rusk doubted Japan's willingness to
aid in its own defense.   He did not share the
optimism of Pentagon planners regarding Japanese
military involvment, since he equated Tokyo's
nonparticipation in the Korean War with resis-
tance to remilitarization even in the face of
external attack.
     In a personal interview, Rusk referred to
Japan's schizophrenia on strategic issues.   The
Japanese, he said, wished to have U.S. military
protection but not to accept or contribute the
forces necessary for defense.   In making his
point Rusk gave the analogy of the man who
wanted to sleep with a woman one night without
having to say hello to her in public the next
day.   He felt the Japanese wanted to have it
both ways.   Despite promises to accept united
command, Rusk doubted whether Japan would assist
in its own defense, let alone accept American
military leadership [Rusk].   In his view, united
command was both irrelevant and impractical.
     On the other two issues--U.S. base rights and
legal immunities--Rusk stood tough.   As for base
rights, the American negotiator's hard-line attitude would eventually force Okazaki to accept
a solution which he felt opposed the nation's
interests.   Tokyo's unhappiness resulted from
the inability to jump the gap in two-party
objectives.   Okazaki clearly believed his goal
to be political.   He wished to show the Japanese
Diet and public that America's use of "installa-

tions and areas" depended on a voluntary grant
of permission from the Japanese government
[Nishimura (a)]. Okazaki wanted not only to
reduce the large number of Occupation facilities
to a smaller figure but also to prove to domestic critics that American forces could not seize
or use property without restriction. The absence of Japanese control, he feared, would
heighten domestic dissatisfaction over a de
facto Occupation after peace.

Rusk, in contrast, defined his goal in strategic terms. He wanted to maintain America's position in East Asia through an automatic right
to use base areas in Japan. As one JCS document
noted, the security arrangements with Japan,
Australia, New Zealand, and the Philippines
"provide the most [security] that we can obtain
in [the] Far East now until [the] Soviet-Commun-
ist China threat ceases."[30]

While the Japanese formulated several ingeni-
ous proposals, they failed to overcome this
basic difference in Tokyo-Washington purpose.
On January 30, 1952, the Japanese first raised
their objections to Article 2 of the American
draft, which provided for the right of U.S.
forces to use installatioins and areas without
interruption until a joint committee of experts
had reached an agreement.[31] The Japanese argued
for deletion, stressing the demise of Occupa-
tion-time relations and the emergence of a new
post-treaty order. America's ability to use
Japanese installations and areas, Okazaki and
Nishimura emphasized, had derived from U.S.
authority as occupying power. Because that
authority would cease when the peace treaty came
into effect, America would have to ask an independent Japan to extend U.S. base rights in the
post-treaty period. In their view, both governments should begin joint committee negotiations
and wrap up an agreement before the treaty's
effective date [Nishimura (a)].

During the meeting, Rusk stressed American and
SCAP desires to return many installations and
areas to Japan before then; he added that any
post-treaty decision would of course be based on
two-party consent. Nevertheless, he argued that
America must have some guarantee on usage in
case the two sides failed to reach an agreement
before the effective date.[32]

The Japanese shot back that agreement could be
reached if the two countries began discussions
immediately. Certainly, they said, Japan would
be glad to support the American position should
Tokyo and Washington hit a snag during talks.
In the meantime, Okazaki warned, the United
States must take care not to arouse Japanese ill
will. As one example, he cited Japanese protest
over America's seizure of several harbor areas
in late 1951.

On February 3 Rusk presented a counterproposal
that offered a statement of U.S. intentions to
end property takeovers and called for an accord
on installations and areas over which agreement
had not been reached by then.

The inspiration for this "escape clause" came
from the peace treaty provision stipulating the
removal of Occupation forces ninety days after
the effective date. Rusk feared that the inability to settle the base issue within that
time would necessitate the removal of U.S.
forces from areas over which agreement had not
been reached.[33] In Rusk's view, Japanese insistence on agreement meant that disagreement would
damage the American strategic position in Japan.
In this sense, the escape clause was an attempt
to force the burden of agreement on Japan by
narrowing its choice to voluntary assent before
the effective date or automatic concession
afterward.

Pleased with neither of these choices, Okazaki
and Nishimura tried a diplomatic end run. In a
statement, they said the Japanese government did

not intend to expel U.S. forces from Japan; it
merely wished to show the Diet and the Japanese
people that a fair solution could be achieved by
mutual agreement.[34]

On February 7, the Japanese representatives
offered a plan which they felt would eliminate
the need for an escape clause. It provided for
the immediate start of bilateral talks with an
initial review of installations located near
metropolitan areas, and the promise to end talks
with an agreement over all installations no
later than ninety days after the effective date
of the peace treaty.

Rusk promised to study the proposal, but his
facial expression betrayed what his response
would be. On February 8, the chief U.S. delegate stated his unhappiness over the proposal.
He first mentioned the irregularity of placing a
provision on timing in an executive agreement
before that agreement had come into effect
[Rusk].[35] Rusk then stated his dissatisfaction
over a mere promise to conclude an arrangement
within ninety days, and he stressed the need to
provide for the uninterrupted use of military
installations and areas over which agreement
could not be reached.

Okazaki bristled. He argued both governments
could easily reach an agreement on all base
areas. After all, they had some four months
before the peace treaty would take effect.
Surely, that would be enough time.

Japanese planners later sent Rusk another
statement underscoring Japanese intentions to
conclude an agreement within ninety days. Rusk,
however, remained unpersuaded. He repeated that
America must have some formal assurance regarding military installations in Japan, and on
February 13 asked for an exchange of documents
acknowledging America's right to use bases without interruption.[36]

It became obvious to Okazaki and Nishimura

that promises of a timely agreement were not
enough. Despite their intention to show their
diplomatic grit, both men soon accepted Rusk's
demand for an escape clause. On February 14 or
15, the chief U.S. delegate, showing Okazaki and
Nishimura a telegram from Truman instructing him
not to yield on the issue, asked the two Japanese for some compromise formula that would satisfy the presidential mandate.[37]

Because the Japanese realized that only a formula that compromised their position would
please Truman and Rusk, Nishimura asked Rusk for
a letter stating American wishes on an escape
clause. He suggested that the Japanese government would accede to the principle of continuous
use by "taking note" of the letter. The Nishimura proposal not only reflected the need to
conclude an executive accord but also indicated
his unhappiness over the particular cost [Nishi-
mura (a)]. As he explained, "Standard procedure
would have been for both governments to place
their views and objections on an escape clause
in the same letter." Nishimura, however, asked
for a separate letter from the United States.
He felt that acceptance of the escape clause so
compromised the nation's territorial integrity
that he wished to minimize Japan's association
with it. In the words of the Treaty Bureau director: "It was that repulsive to us" [Nishimura
(a)].

On February 15 Okazaki explained the situation
to Yoshida and asked for approval of the Nishimura proposal. The prime minister agreed, apparently feeling that Japan had no choice in the
matter after White House intervention. Nevertheless, Yoshida wished to make clear in Article
2 that installations and areas used by Occupation troops would in principle revert to Japan
upon peace and that their subsequent use would
nominally depend upon mutual agreement.

The final text of Article 2 was a superficial

half-victory of sorts. Even though it did not
include the principle of reversion, Article 2
incorporated the element of mutual agreement.
In the Japanese view, it thus added a glitter of
equality to an otherwise unequal accord.

Besides base rights, Tokyo officials fought a
second losing battle. That clash involved the
right of Japanese courts to exercise criminal
jurisdiction over U.S. military and civilian
personnel in Japan. Okazaki, Yoshida, and Nishimura felt criminal jurisdiction to be the most
important of the three issues. They again wanted to avoid the appearance of a post-treaty Occupation and therefore struggled against an ex-
tension of U.S. legal immunities after peace.
As Nishimura remarked, "It was unbearable that
American forces and their families be allowed to
keep their special immunities from criminal pro-
secution after independence. Under the Occupation, police and judicial powers over those per-
sons were left to U.S. military police and
courts. Japan had no authority over them and
was uncertain which laws the courts would apply"
[Nishimura (a)].

Their strong feelings caused Japanese leaders
to applaud the NATO Status of Forces Agreement,
which recognized host state jurisdiction in two
cases: (1) where a member of the visiting
state's contingent committed an offense that
violated the law of the host state but not of
the visiting state, and (2) where members of the
visiting state's contingent committed an offense
that violated the law of both states and occurred outside the performance of official duty.[38]

But the American proposal submitted by Rusk in
late January departed from that precedent. It
not only stipulated U.S. military powers of arrest outside base areas but also gave American
authorities exclusive jurisdiction over U.S.
personnel for all crimes committed in Japan.
U.S. tribunals would thus have primary jurisdiction even when Americans committed crimes

against Japanese outside base areas during off-
duty hours.
   The U.S. proposal did contain a safety device,
though. It offered to apply SOFA if Congress
passed NATO one year after the administrative
agreement came into effect, and, moreover, proposed to reconsider criminal jurisdiction if
Congress failed to ratify NATO by then [Rusk].
Still, the Japanese were not satisfied.
   During the first secret session, Okazaki objected to the American calls for exclusive jurisdiction and delay in resorting to SOFA. The
Japanese representative argued that the Status
of Forces Agreement should be used immediately
because it stood on the principle of equality.
Okazaki then said he recognized the difficulty
of applying a collective defense to an unarmed
Japan. Nevertheless, he continued, the principle of equality was so important that it should
be incorporated into the bilateral relationship.[39]
   Rusk returned the fire, maintaining that SOFA
could not be applied because Congress had not
yet approved the North Atlantic Treaty. The
U.S. negotiator further stressed that the document was experiencing difficulty and its ratification could not be presumed. Meanwhile, both
countries should adopt the U.S.-U.K. wartime
agreement governing American forces in Great
Britain.
   Okazaki objected. He contended the criminal
jurisdiction provisions of that accord had sur-
rendered British sovereignty to the United
States, and asked whether the United Kingdom had
not demanded revision after the war. Okazaki
then pointed to the U.S.-Philippine base agreement permitting limited host state jurisdiction
over American forces. In his opinion, the government could not easily explain to the Japanese
why their administrative agreement should be
inferior to the U.S.-Philippine accord.
   During their second meeting, Rusk reaffirmed

America's intention to apply the NATO formula to
Japan in the future. But he also stressed the
illogic of using SOFA in Japan before the Senate[40]
passed NATO and applied it to Western Europe.
Such action, Rusk hinted, would treat a defeated
enemy better than a wartime ally.
      Upon hearing this statement, Japanese repre-
sentatives concluded that Rusk would never agree
to apply SOFA immediately to Japan. Okazaki and
Nishimura consequently changed the direction of
their negotiating efforts. On the technical
staff level, they had lower-ranking officials
try to qualify U.S. rights by refinements in
language and arguments based on international
law.
      During one staff meeting, Japanese negotiators
asked for several changes, including the re-
placement of "U.S. military forces" with a sof-
ter reference to "U.S. authorities," and the
limitation of U.S. powers of arrest to sabotage[41]
and spying against American bases in Japan.
      Japanese represenatives also asked for the
deletion of the most embarrassing portion of the
U.S. proposal—namely, the call for American
primary jurisdiction over all base personnel for
all crimes committed in Japan. They argued international legal custom supported the general
principle that immunities of a visiting military
force attached to location, not to person. Japanese courts should thus be granted authority in
cases where members of the U.S. contingent committed crimes against Japanese citizens outside
base areas. American representatives refused to
discuss the last point, contending that it
should be brought up to the Rusk-Okazaki level
for review [Fujisaki].
      Several days later Japanese delegates reiter-
ated their requests for language changes and
objections to primary jurisdiction by the United
States. They also elaborated on Okazaki's earlier criticism of the U.S.-U.K. wartime agree-

ment. In their view, it had been signed during
the Second World War when America truly needed
to keep control over its own forces. The Japanese representatives, mentioning the Philippine
government's jurisdiction under its base agreement with America, warned of domestic protest
against U.S. legal immunities in Japan after
peace.[42]

This time the Americans came better prepared.
They stressed that the unusual circumstances of
the Occupation could not be changed overnight;
some intermediate step would be needed before
Japan could exercise legal jursidiction. The
U.S. negotiators then set off a salvo in defense
of the Philippine accord, pointedly reminding
the Japanese of American-Filipino trust and
friendship before the war.

Disappointed by continued U.S. stubbornness,
Tokyo officials decided to end their efforts on
behalf of host state jurisdiction. During his
next session with Rusk, Okazaki asked for several minor changes to lessen the sting of America's legal monopoly--including a Washington
pledge to report the decisions of U.S. military
courts and to consider Japanese requests for
jurisdiction.[43] Rusk agreed.

Throughout the talks, the Japanese hoped that
appeals to fairness would persuade Rusk. They
judged that SOFA, international law, and the
U.S.-Philippine base accord would provide them
with enough ammunition to shoot down American
legal privilege in Japan [Nishimura (a)]. Unfortunately for them, though, fairness had
little to do with Rusk's opposition to Japanese
jursidiction. Certainly, Rusk and the American
negotiating team offered carefully crafted arguments linked to legal and policy considerations.
Their real reasons, however, were quite
different.

Despite the orderliness of the past six years,
Rusk and others feared that a Japan just out of

Occupation could become imbued with a spirit of
retribution toward her occupiers. Japanese pro-
secutors might therefore apply the law arbitrar-
ily in order to make U.S. soldiers the symbols
against whom national ill will could be vented.
Moreover, Rusk and his associates honestly considered themselves to be ignorant of Japanese
culture and law. This unfamiliarity with an
alien tradition and legal system only increased
their anxiety about subjecting American soldiers
to Japanese justice [Rusk]. Given Truman's
instructions to approximate the NATO accord,
Rusk apparently looked on the one-year delay as
a period during which the depth of Japanese
friendship could be measured and the desirability of applying SOFA could be appraised.

5

A FINAL WORD

Japanese planning on the San Francisco Peace
Settlement revealed an alliance in emergence as
well as an issue in transition. Throughout the
Occupation, Tokyo leaders stitched together a
series of accords that would protect Japan's
vital interests. While the designs varied, the
fabric remained the same.

Responding to internal need and external circumstances, Japanese officials formulated policies whose success depended on U.S. support.
In their view, American dominance of the Western alliance made the United States the logical
guarantor of Japan's long-term survival. Iden-
tifying strategic, political, and economic
objectives in terms of the United States, Tokyo
planners pursued their aims in a way that would
consolidate the Japanese-American relationhip
itself.

While accepting the ground rule of Washington
leadership, Japanese officials played a peace
treaty and foreign relations game with the
cards stacked in favor of America. From the
latter half of the Occupation, Japanese leaders
shifted attention from a nonpunitive peace,
U.S. protection, and other substantive concerns
to demands reflecting the desire for new diplomatic status. Requests for an equal security
treaty, legal jurisdiction over U.S. servicemen, ties to Communist China, and self-deter-
mination on military buildup pinpointed wishes
for a more independent pro-American path. In
the view of senior officials, Japan's strategic
location and industrial potential would enable
them to establish the partnership that would
win public support and satisfy their personal
desires.

Washington disagreed, however. From a different reading of Japan's importance, U.S.
leaders favored policies guaranteeing independence consistent with American strategic objectives in the Far East. Their calls for a re-
armed Japan, Tokyo-Taipei ties, and U.S. military control cut sharply against the grain of
Japanese objectives.

Tokyo officials grudgingly accepted, for,
apart from China policy, they felt they had no
choice. Opposition would endanger the pros-
pects of peace; what was more important, it
could unravel the new relationship with America. As a result, Japanese leaders signed a
series of agreements riddled with inequality.
In their view, a peace treaty falling outside
the United Nations Charter, a security treaty
omitting mutuality, and an administrative accord affirming American control punctuated
imbalance in Tokyo-Washington ties. For the
moment, the Japanese would have to bite the
diplomatic bullet. But perhaps, sometime in
the future, they might try to reshape an alliance under Occupation.

NOTES

1

EARLY PLANNING FOR A PEACE CONFERENCE, 1945-1947

1. Kumao Nishimura, Nihon Gaikoshi, p. 27. See
   also "Interview with General of the Army
   Douglas MacArthur," in Foreign Relations of
   the United States, 1946, 8:115-26.
2. See also "Senkajin Tanko Rodosha Mondai ni
   Kansuru Hokkaido Shutcho Hokokusho," in
   Koichiro Asakai, Hokokusho Shuroku.
3. See also "Tochiken no Seigen," in Kyuman Suzuki, Nihon Gaikoshi (Tokyo: Kajima Shup-
   pankai, 1970), 26:111-15.
4. Nishimura, Nihon Gaikoshi, pp. 29-32.
5. "Interview with Press Correspondents, March
   19, 1947," in Report of the Government
   Section, Political Reorientation of Japan:
   September 1945-September 1948 (Grosse
   Pointe, Mich.: Scholarly Press, 19xx),
   1:765-66.
6. "Memorandum by the Deputy Director of the
   Office of Far Eastern Affairs," in FRUS,
   1947, 6:476.
7. Nishimura, Nihon Gaikoshi, pp. 32-33.
8. Kumao Nishimura, "Senryo Zenki," p. 77.
9. Ibid., p. 78.
10. See also "Introduction," in Kyuman Suzuki,
    Nihon Gaikoshi, p. 5.
11. Nishimura, "Senryo Zenki," pp. 77-78.
12. Ibid.
13. "Memorandum by the Secretary of State to the
    President, February 27, 1946," in FRUS,
    1946, 8:151. See also "Draft Treaty on the
    Disarmament and Demilitarization of Japan,"
    in FRUS, 1946, 8:151-55.

14. "Smith to the Secretary of State, July 23, 1947," in FRUS, 1947, 6:473-74.
15. "Memorandum by Counselor of the Department to Under Secretary of State, August 12, 1947," in FRUS, 1947, 6:487.
16. "Memorandum of Conversation with Tsarapkin and Thompson," in FRUS, 1947, 6:491-92.
17. See also "Memorandum by Davies, August 11, 1947," and "Notation by Lovett," in FRUS, 1947, 6:486-87.
18. Developments Toward Formulation of U.S. Policy with Respect to a Japanese Peace Settlement, MacArthur Papers, MacArthur Memorial Library, Norfolk, Va.
19. Ibid.
20. Eichelberger diary, entry for June 26, 1947.
21. Eichelberger diary, entry for September 10, 1947.
22. The text appears in Ikuhiko Hata, Shiroku, pp. 206-208.
23. Hata, Shiroku, pp. 206-208.
24. Ibid.
25. Nishimura, Nihon Gaikoshi, p. 39.
26. "Memorandum of Conversation by Sebald, 26 October 1947," in FRUS, 1947, 6:547.
27. "Memorandum of Conversation with Chief Cabinet Secretary and the Speaker of the House of Representatives, 5 November 1947," Department of State File: 894, National Archives, Washington.
28. Ibid.
29. "Memorandum of Conversation with the Vice Minister of Foreign Affairs, 22 December 1947," Department of State File: 740.0011, National Archives, Washington.
30. "Tokyo's Secret Plans for Peace," World Report (December 9, 1947), 3(24):18, 19, 33-36.
31. "Memorandum of Conversation with the Vice Minister of Foreign Affairs, 22 December 1947."

2

THE YOSHIDA INITIATIVE, 1948-1950

1. "Report by the Director of the Policy Planning Staff [Kennan]:   Recommendations with
   Respect to US Policy Toward Japan, March 25,
   1948," in Foreign Relations of the United
   States, 1948, 6:691-719.
2. "Secretary of State to Certain Diplomatic
   Offices, 27 April 1949," in FRUS, 1949,
   7(2):717-20.
3. Gaimusho, ed., Kokkai Ni Okeru Kowa Rongi,
   pp. 151-52.
4. Ibid., pp. 196, 202.
5. Ibid., p. 177.
6. "Memorandum by the Director of the Office of
   Far Eastern Affairs [Butterworth] to the
   Under Secretary of State [Webb], 19 May
   1949," in FRUS, 1949, 7(2):752-54; and
   "Memoranda by the Chief of the Division of
   Northeast Asian Affairs, 18 February 1949,"
   in FRUS, 1949, 7(2):659-63.
7. Gaimusho, Kokkai Ni Okeru Kowa Rongi, p.
   283.
8. Ibid., p. 299.
9. Ibid., p. 314.
10. "Memorandum by the JCS to the Secretary of
    Defense, 22 December 1949," in FRUS, 1949,
    7(2):922-23.
11. "Memorandum of Conversation by the Special
    Assistant to the Secretary, 24 April 1950,"
    in FRUS, 1950, 6:1175-82.
12. Dean Acheson, Present at the Creation, p.
    431.
13. Ibid.
14. Ibid.
15. Akahata, October 9, 1949. See also "Kowa
    Mondai to Nihon Kyosanto," in Zen'ei,
    January 1950.
16. Sekai, March 1950.
17. Nihon Shakaito, Nijyunen no Kiroku, pp. 109-
    10.

18. Asahi Shimbun, November 2, 1949, and May 21, 1950.
19. Kiichi Miyazawa, Tokyo-Washington no Mitsu-dan, pp. 39-40.
20. Ibid.
21. Memorandum of the Dodge-Ikeda Conversation, May 3, 1950, MacArthur Papers, Norfolk, Va.
22. Ibid.
23. Ibid.
24. Miyazawa, Tokyo-Washington no Mitsudan, pp. 64-69.

3

THE DULLES-YOSHIDA
SECURITY NEGOTIATIONS, 1950-1951

1. See also "Memorandum of Conversation by the Special Assistant with the Secretary, 7 April 1950," in Foreign Relations of the United States, 1950, 6:1165.
2. Interview with William Sebald, Dulles Oral History Collection, Princeton University.
3. Kumao Nishimura, Nihon Gaikoshi, pp. 80-81.
4. Ibid.
5. Kumao Nishimura, Anzen Hosho Joyakuron, p. 27.
6. "Memorandum by the Officer in Charge of Japanese Affairs, August 2, 1950," in FRUS, 1950, 6:1262-64.
7. Nishimura, Anzen Hosho Joyakuron, p. 27.
8. Nishimura, Nihon Gaikoshi, pp. 86-87.
9. Ibid., pp. 87-88.
10. Ibid.
11. Interview with Prime Minister Shigeru Yoshida, National Diet Library, Tokyo.
12. Nishimura, Nihon Gaikoshi, pp. 87-88. See also Martin E. Weinstein, Japan's Postwar Defense Policy, pp. 60-63.
13. Interview with Sebald.
14. Ibid. See also Interview with Yoshida.
15. Interview with Sebald.

16. "Memorandum by Dulles to Acheson, 19 July
    1950," in FRUS, 1950, 6:1243-44; and untit-
    led memorandum by Dulles, July 6, 1950,
    Dulles Papers, Princeton University.
17. To the Secretary from Mr. Dulles, November
    30, 1950, Dulles Papers, Princeton Univer-
    sity.
18. Letter from Dulles to MacArthur, December
    20, 1950, MacArthur papers, Norfolk, Va.
19. "Conversation between MacArthur and Kennan,
    21 March 1948," in FRUS, 1948, 6:708-709.
20. Interview with Yoshida.
21. "Memorandum of Conversation by the Special
    Assistant to the Secretary," in FRUS, 1950,
    6:1165.
22. The Foreign Ministry record of the security
    treaty and rearmament plan negotiations
    appears in the Tokyo Shimbun, May 13, 1977.
    Nishimura confirmed the authenticity of the
    record in his personal interview (June 20,
    1977).
23. Ibid.
24. Nishimura, Nihon Gaikoshi, pp. 91-92.
25. Tokyo Shimbun, May 13, 1977.
26. Ibid. (writer's translation of the original
    document)
27. Nishimura, Nihon Gaikoshi, pp. 92-93.
28. Tokyo Shimbun, May 13, 1977.
29. Ibid.
30. Interview with a high-ranking American
    official.

4

THE PRICE OF RATIFICATION, 1951-1952

1. "Memorandum of Conversation with Huston, April 8, 1950," in Foreign Relations of the
   United States, 1950, 6:1166-67.
2. Kumao Nishimura, Nihon Gaikoshi, pp. 112-13.
   See also "Memoranda of Conversations by

Robert A. Fearey, April 18, 1951," in FRUS, 1951, 6(1):984-86.
3. See also "Memorandum of Conversation by Robert A. Fearey, April 23, 1951," in FRUS, 1951, 6(1):1316.
4. Nishimura, Nihon Gaikoshi, pp. 191-92.
5. Yomiuri Shimbun (evening edition), October 29, 1951.
6. Nishimura, Nihon Gaikoshi, p. 313.
7. Asahi Shimbun, December 11, 1951.
8. Interview with William Sebald, Dulles Oral History Collection, Princeton University. See also "Memorandum by Sebald, December 13, 1951," in FRUS, 1951, 6(1):1437-39.
9. Ibid.
10. Nishimura, Nihon Gaikoshi, p. 315.
11. Interview with Sebald.
12. See also "Memorandum of Conversation between Senator H. Alexander Smith and Prime Minister Shigeru Yoshida, December 18, 1951," in FRUS, 1951, 6(1):1447-48.
13. See also "Memorandum of Conversation by Dean Rusk," in FRUS, 1951, 6(1):1416.
14. Nishimura, Nihon Gaikoshi, p. 316.
15. Interview with Sebald.
16. Ibid. See also "Memorandum by Sebald, December 18, 1951," in FRUS, 1951, 6(1):1444.
17. See also "Memorandum by Sebald, December 18, 1951," p. 1444.
18. See also Interview with Sebald.
19. See also "Interview with Ambassador John M. Allison," in Minoru Omori, Sengo Mitsushi, p. 273.
20. Chae-Jin Lee, Japan Faces China, p. 28.
21. Nishimura, Nihon Gaikoshi, pp. 327-28.
22. Shigeru Yoshida, Kaiso Junen, 3:127-28.
23. Memorandum of Conversation between Dulles and Acheson, 22 October 1951, Dulles Papers, Princeton University.
24. "JCS Records: Japanese Peace Treaty File, 22 January 1952," National Archives,Washington.

25. Memorandum of Conversation between Dulles and Acheson, 22 October 1951.
26. Draft Peace Treaty, February 11, 1951, MacArthur Papers, Norfolk, Va.
27. See also Nishimura, Anzen Hosho Joyakuron, pp. 93-95.
28. Yoshida, Kaiso Junen, p. 141.
29. Nishimura, Anzen Hosho Joyakuron.
30. "JCS Records: Japanese Peace Treaty File, 22 January 1952," National Archives, Washington.
31. Nishimura, Nihon Gaikoshi, p. 338.
32. Ibid., p. 340.
33. Ibid., p. 344.
34. Nishimura, Anzen Hosho Joyakuron, p. 92.
35. Nishimura, Nihon Gaikoshi, pp. 349-50.
36. Ibid., pp. 341-42.
37. Ibid., p. 346.
38. Ibid., pp. 349-50.
39. Ibid.
40. Ibid., pp. 350-51.
41. Ibid., pp. 351-52.
42. Ibid., pp. 352-55.
43. Ibid.

BIBLIOGRAPHY

PERSONAL INTERVIEWS

Ambassador John ALLISON, director of the Office of Far Eastern Affairs (August 13, 1977).

Dr. Hugh BORTON, State Department acting chief of the Division of Japanese Affairs, 1946 (December 13, 1979).

Supreme Court Justice Masato FUJISAKI (March 28, 1977).

Ambassador Toru HAGIWARA, Treaty Bureau director, 1946-1947 (March 24, 1977).

Dr. Kenzo KAWAKAMI, member of the Hagiwara Group and author of the territories reference documents, 1947-1950 (June 6, 1977).

Minister Kiichi MIYAZAWA, personal secretary to Ikeda Hayato, 1950 (March 29, 1977).

Kazuo NAKAJIMA, personal secretary to Katsuo Okazaki, Ministry of Foreign Affairs (April 1, 1977).

Ambassador Kumao NISHIMURA (a), Treaty Bureau staff member, 1946; Treaty Bureau director, 1947-1952 (February 2, 1977).

Ambassador NISHIMURA (b) (June 20, 1977).

Dr. Ralph REID, personal secretary to Joseph Dodge (June 17, 1977).

Dean RUSK, assistant secretary of state for the Far East, 1951-1952 (February 26, 1978).

Ambassador Takezo SHIMODA, Treaty Bureau deputy director, 1946 (June 14, 1977).

Ambassador Kyuman SUZUKI, director of the Central Liaison Office in Yokohama, 1947 (February 9, 1977).

Ambassador Michitoshi TAKAHASHI, of the Central Liaison Office, 1946; Treaty Bureau deputy director, 1950 (March 4, 1977).

Eiichi TATSUMI, confidential military affairs advisor to Shigeru Yoshida, 1946-1952 (June 6, 1977).

Torao USHIROKU, member of the Hagiwara Group and
author of the domestic police force reference
documents, 1946 (March 4, 1977).

JAPANESE LANGUAGE MATERIALS

Akahata (1949-1950).
Asahi Shimbun (1945-1952).
Asakai Koichiro. Hokokusho Shuroku. Foreign
    Ministry Archives, Tokyo.
Gaimusho, ed.   Kokkai Ni Okeru Kowa Rongi.
    Tokyo: Gaimusho, 1951.
Hata Ikuhiko. Shiroku: Nihon Saigunbi. Tokyo:
    Bungei Shunju, 1976.
Katayama Tetsu. Kaiko to Tenbo. Tokyo: Fuku-
    mura Shuppan, 1967.
Kokkai Toshokan, ed., "Yoshida Soridaijin no
    Intabyu."   Tokyo: Kokkai Toshokan, 1956.
    Declassified in 1977.
Mainichi Shimbun (1945-1952).
Miyazawa Kiichi.   Tokyo-Washington no Mitsudan.
    Tokyo: Jitsugyo no Nihonsha, 1956.
Nihon Shakaito.   Nijyunen no Kiroku.   Tokyo:
    Nihon Shakaito, 1965.
Nishimura Kumao. Anzen Hosho Joyakuron. Tokyo:
    Jiji Tsushinsha, 1959.
--Nihon Gaikoshi, vol. 27. Tokyo: Kajima
    Shuppankai, 1970.
--"Senryo Zenki no Tainichi Kowai Mondai."   In
    The Finance (February 1975), 10(11):77-83.
Omori Minoru. Sengo Mitsushi, vol. 9. Tokyo:
    Yomiuri, 1977.
Seizaburo Shinobu. Sengo Nihon Seijishi, 1945--
    1952, vols. 1-4. Tokyo: Keiso Shobo, 1967.
Suzuki Kyuman, ed., Nihon Gaikoshi, vol. 26.
    Tokyo: Kajima Shuppankai, 1970.
Tatsumi Eiichi.   "Saigunbi ni Hantai Shita
    Yoshida Shigeru." In Toki no Kadai. Tokyo:
    Toki no Kadai, 1963.
Tokyo Shimbun (1977).

Watanabe Takeshi. Senryoka no Nihon Zaisei
    Oboegaki. Tokyo: Nihon Keizai Shinbunsha,
    1961.
Yomiuri Shimbun (1945-1952).
Yoshida Shigeru. Kaiso Junen, vols. 1-4.
    Tokyo: Shinahosha, 1957-1958.
Zen'ei (1949-1950).

ENGLISH LANGUAGE MATERIALS

Acheson, Dean. Present at the Creation. New
    York: Norton, 1967.
Allison, John M. Ambassador from the Prairie,
    or Allison Wonderland. Boston: Houghton
    Mifflin, 1973.
Auer, James E. The Postwar Rearmament of Japan-
    ese Maritime Forces, 1945-1971. New York:
    Praeger, 1973.
Dower, John W. Empire and Aftermath: Yoshida
    Shigeru and the Japanese Experience, 1878-
    1954. Cambridge, Mass.: Council on East
    Asian Studies, Harvard University, 1979.
John Foster Dulles Papers and Oral History Col-
    lection. Princeton University.
Eichelberger, Robert. Eichelberger Diary. Duke
    University, Durham, N.C.
Fearey, Robert A. The Occupation of Japan, Sec-
    ond Phase: 1948-1950. Westport, Conn.:
    Greenwood Press, 1972.
Fukui, Haruhiro. Party in Power: The Japanese
    Liberal-Democrats and Policy-Making. Ber-
    keley: University of California Press, 1970.
Guhin, Michael A. John Foster Dulles: A States-
    man and His Times. New York: Columbia Uni-
    versity Press, 1972.
Hadley, Eleanor M. Antitrust in Japan. Prince-
    ton: Princeton University Press, 1972.
Hinton, Harold C. Three and a Half Powers: The
    New Balance in Asia. Bloomington: Indiana
    University Press, 1975.

Iriye, Akira. The Cold War in Asia: A Histori-
cal Introduction.   Englewood Cliffs, N.J.:
Prentice-Hall, 1974.
Kesavan, K. V. Japan's Relations with Southeast
Asia, 1952-1969. Bombay: Somaiya Publica-
tions, 1972.
Lee, Chae-Jin.   Japan Faces China: Political
and Economic Relations in the Postwar Era.
Baltimore: Johns Hopkins University Press,
1976.
MacArthur Papers.   General Douglas MacArthur
Memorial Library, Norfolk, Va.
Manchester, William R. American Caesar: Doug-
las MacArthur, 1880-1964.   Boston: Little,
Brown, 1978.
Martin, Edwin M. The Allied Occupation of Japan.
Westport, Conn.: Greenwood Press, 1972.
Masataka Kosaka.   100 Million Japanese: The
Postwar Experience. Tokyo: Kodansha Interna-
tional, 1972.
Mendl, Wolf.   Issues in Japan's China Policy.
London: Macmillan, for the Royal Institute of
International Affairs, 1978.
Minear, Richard H. Victors' Justice: The Tokyo
War Crimes Trial.   Princeton: Princeton
University Press, 1971.
Nihon Kyosanto. The Fifty Years of the Commun-
ist Party of Japan. Tokyo: Central Committee
of the Communist Party of Japan, 1973.
Olson, Lawrence.   Japan in Postwar Asia.   New
York: Praeger, for the Council on Foreign
Relations, 1970.
Redford, L. H., ed.   The Occupation of Japan.
Norfolk, Va.:   General Douglas MacArthur
Memorial Library, 1976.
Swearingen, Rodger.   The Soviet Union and Post-
war Japan: Escalating Challenge and Response.
Stanford, Calif.:   Hoover Institution Press,
1978.
U.S. Department of State.   Foreign Relations of
the United States: 1946 (vol. 8), 1947 (vol.

6), <u>1948</u> (vol. 6), <u>1949</u> (vol. 7), <u>1950</u> (vol. 6), and <u>1951</u> (vol. 6). Washington: GPO, 1971-1977.
U.S. Department of State. <u>Japanese Occupation and Peace Treaty File, 1952.</u> National Archives, Washington.
U.S. Joint Chiefs of Staff. <u>Japanese Peace Treaty File, 1952.</u> National Archives, Washington.
Vishwanathan, Savitri. <u>Normalization of Japanese-Soviet Relations, 1945-1970.</u> Tallahassee, Fla.: Diplomatic Press, 1973.
Ward, Robert E. <u>Japan's Political System.</u> 2d ed. Englewood Cliffs, N.J.: Prentice-Hall, 1978.
--"The Legacy of the Occupation." In Herbert Passin, ed., <u>The United States and Japan.</u> 2d ed., rev. Washington: Columbia Books, 1975.
Watanabe, Akio. <u>The Okinawa Problem: A Chapter in Japan-United States Relations.</u> Carlton, Australia: Melbourne University Press, 1970.
Weinstein, Martin E. <u>Japan's Postwar Defense Policy, 1947-1968.</u> New York: Columbia University Press, 1971.
Whitney, Courtney. <u>MacArthur: His Rendezvous with History.</u> Westport, Conn.: Greenwood Press, 1977.
Wittner, Laurence S., ed. <u>MacArthur.</u> Englewood Cliffs, N.J.: Prentice-Hall, 1971.
Yoshida Shigeru. <u>The Yoshida Memoirs: The Story of Japan in Crisis.</u> Westport, Conn.: Greenwood Press, 1973.

INDEX

A

Acheson, Dean, 28-30, 55, 70, 74
The Allied Council, 1, 3, 8, 12
Allison, John M., 31, 41, 42, 50, 55, 57-60, 63,
   63, 65, 66, 83
America, 6, 32, 37, 48, 49, 52, 54, 74, 97
Asakai, Koichiro, 8
Asanuma, Inejiro, 42
Ashida, Hitoshi, 8-12, 16-23
Atcheson, George, 7, 10, 11, 17
Australia, 10, 12, 13, 90

B

Babcock, Stanton, 57
Ball, MacMahon, 8, 12
Bohlen, Charles, 13
Bonin Islands, 4, 9, 19, 44, 45, 54, 64
Borton Committee, 3, 12, 13
Butterworth, Walter, 28
Byrnes, James, 1, 13, 16

C

Chiang Kai-shek, 68, 74, 82
Clay, Lucius, 56
Communist China, 28, 41, 43, 52, 53, 67
Communist Party of Japan, 5, 6, 21, 26-28, 31,
   32

D

Democratic Party of Japan, 8
Dodge, Joseph, 33, 34, 37, 45
Draper, William, 21, 34 37
Dulles, John Foster, 34, 40, 41, 42, 47, 50-52,
    54, 56, 57, 62, 64-66, 69, 70, 73, 75-78, 82,
    85

E

Eden, Anthony, 79
Eichelberger, Robert, 14, 15, 17-19, 31, 34
Evatt, Herbert, 12

F

The Far Eastern Council, 3, 9, 12, 13, 43
France, 3
Fujisaki Masato, 48, 49

G

Gascoigne, Alvary D. F., 21
Great Britain, 3, 74

H

Hagiwara Group, 1-7, 8, 10
Hagiwara, Toru, 1, 4, 17, 23
Hokkaido, 1

I

Iguchi, Sadao, 57-59, 62-65, 73, 83
Ikeda, Hayato, 33-35
Italy, 2, 6

J

Joint Chiefs of Staff, 29, 30, 55, 85, 90
Johnson, Earl, 57-59, 63, 64
Johnson, Louis, 29-31

K

Katayama, Tetsu, 8, 12, 18, 20-22
Kennan, George, 25, 55
Kimura, Shiroshichi, 79, 81, 82
Korean War, 42, 45, 52
Kurile Islands, 3, 4, 7, 9, 12, 18, 25, 35, 39,
    44, 45

L

Lawrence, W. Henry, 22

M

MacArthur, Douglas, 8, 15, 22, 30, 33, 37, 50-
    52, 55, 56, 64
Magruder, Carter, 57, 63, 65
Marshall, George, 14, 25
Miyazawa, Kiichi, 34
Molotov, V. M., 12
Moscow, 1, 17, 19, 21, 39

N

Nationalist China, 26, 73, 74, 82
National Police Reserves, 59, 64, 86
New Zealand, 53, 90
Nishimura, Kumao, 43-48, 50, 54-60, 62-65, 72,
    74, 83, 84, 87, 90-94, 96
Nishio, Suehiro, 21, 22

O

Okazaki, Katsuo, 8, 17, 18, 22, 23, 32, 84, 87-
  96, 97
Ota, Ichiro, 17, 45

P

Pacific Pact, 53, 54
Pauley, Edwin, 2, 26
Pauley Report, 4
Peking, 67, 74, 78
Pentagon, 15, 47, 55, 85, 89
People's Republic of China, 69-72, 74, 76, 78,
  82
Potsdam Declaration, 1, 4

R

Reid, Ralph, 34
Republic of China, 72, 77, 79, 80, 82
Ridgway, Matthew, 69
Royall, Kenneth, 35
Rusk, Dean, 42, 85, 87-93, 95-97
Ryukyu Islands, 4, 9, 19, 30, 45, 64, 89

S

Sakhalin, 12, 13, 18, 25, 35
San Francisco Peace Conference, 70, 74
San Francisco Peace Settlement, 74, 75, 77, 80,
  88, 90
Sebald, William, 22, 41, 45, 50, 52, 76
Security Treaty, 47-49, 60
Shaw, Patrick, 21
Smith, Alexander, 72, 73
Smith, W. Bedell, 13
Socialist Party of Japan, 8, 21, 26, 27, 32, 42
Soviet Union, 2, 3, 10, 12, 14, 16, 18, 20, 21,
  23, 25, 29, 30, 39, 41, 43, 52, 55

Sparkman, John, 72, 73
Stalin, Joseph, 41
Status of Forces Agreement, 83, 84, 94-96, 98
Supreme Commander of the Allied Powers, 3, 10,
   36, 37, 91
Suzuki, Kyuman, 15-18

T

Taipei, 74, 79
Taiwan, 53, 71, 75, 77, 78, 80-83
Tatsumi, Eiichi, 40, 49, 50, 61
Truman, Harry S., 69, 85, 93, 98
Tsarapkin, Semen K., 14

U

United Kingdom, 21, 76, 95
United Nations, 9, 14, 19, 31, 32, 43, 45, 52,
   54, 59, 63
U.S. Department of the Army, 35
U.S. Department of Defense, 30, 46, 65
U.S. Department of State, 9, 10, 13, 16, 25, 28,
   30, 37, 43, 46, 55, 65
U.S. Department of War, 35, 43
United States-Philippine Base Agreement, 48, 95,
   97
U.S. Senate, 67, 85
Ushiroku, Torao, 79, 81, 82

V

Voorhees, Tracy, 37

W

Whitney, Courtney, 10, 11, 17
Willoughby, Charles, 40

Y

Yalta, 13
Yoshida, Shigeru, 1, 7, 25-29, 32-47, 49-56, 60-
  62, 64, 65, 71-82
Yoshizawa, Seiijiro, 17

STUDIES OF THE EAST ASIAN INSTITUTE

The Ladder of Success in Imperial China, by
    Ping-ti Ho. New York: Columbia University
    Press, 1962.
The Chinese Inflation, 1937-1949, by Shun-hsin
    Chou. New York: Columbia University Press,
    1963.
Reformer in Modern China: Chang Chien, 1853-
    1926, by Samuel Chu. New York: Columbia
    University Press, 1965.
Research in Japanese Sources: A Guide, by
    Herschel Webb with the assistance of Marleigh
    Ryan. New York: Columbia University Press,
    1965.
Society and Education in Japan, by Herbert Pas-
    sin. New York: Teachers College Press, 1965.
Agricultural Production and Economic Development
    in Japan, 1873-1922, by James I. Nakamura.
    Princeton: Princeton University Press, 1966.
Japan's First Modern Novel: Ukigumo of Futaba-
    tei Shimei, by Marleigh Ryan. New York: Col-
    umbia University Press, 1967.
The Korean Communist Movement, 1918-1948, by
    Dae-Sook Suh. Princeton: Princeton Univer-
    sity Press, 1967.
The First Vietnam Crisis, by Melvin Gurtov. New
    York: Columbia University Press, 1967.
Cadres, Bureaucracy, and Political Power in Com-
    munist China, by A. Doak Barnett. New York:
    Columbia University Press, 1968.
The Japanese Imperial Institution in the Tokuga-
    wa Period, by Herschel Webb. New York: Col-
    umbia University Press, 1968.
Higher Education and Business Recruitment in
    Japan, by Koya Azumi. New York: Teachers
    College Press, 1969.

The Communists and Peasant Rebellions: A Study
in the Rewriting of Chinese History, by James
P. Harrison, Jr. New York: Atheneum, 1969.
How the Conservatives Rule Japan, by Nathaniel
B. Thayer. Princeton: Princeton University
Press, 1969.
Aspects of Chinese Education, edited by C. T.
Hu. New York: Teachers College Press, 1970.
Documents of Korean Communism, 1918-1948, by
Dae-Sook Suh. Princeton: Princeton University Press, 1970.
Japanese Education: A Bibliography of Materials
in the English Language, by Herbert Passin.
New York: Teachers College Press, 1970.
Economic Development and the Labor Market in
Japan, by Koji Taira. New York: Columbia
University Press, 1970.
The Japanese Oligarchy and the Russo-Japanese
War, by Shumpei Okamoto. New York: Columbia
University Press, 1970.
Imperial Restoration in Medieval Japan, by H.
Paul Varley. New York: Columbia University
Press, 1971.
Japan's Postwar Defense Policy, 1947-1968, by
Martin E. Weinstein. New York: Columbia
University Press, 1971.
Election Campaigning Japanese Style, by Gerald
L. Curtis. New York: Columbia University
Press, 1971.
China and Russia: The "Great Game," by O. Edmund Clubb. New York: Columbia University
Press, 1971.
Money and Monetary Policy in Communist China, by
Katharine Huang Hsiao. New York: Columbia
University Press, 1971.
The District Magistrate in Late Imperial China,
by John R. Watt. New York: Columbia University Press, 1972.
Law and Policy in China's Foreign Relations: A
Study of Attitudes and Practice, by James C.
Hsiung. New York: Columbia University Press,
1972.

Pearl Harbor as History: Japanese-American Relations, 1931-1941, edited by Dorothy Borg and Shumpei Okamoto, with the assistance of Dale K. A. Finlayson. New York: Columbia University Press, 1973.

Japanese Culture: A Short History, by H. Paul Varley. New York: Praeger, 1973.

Doctors in Politics: The Political Life of the Japan Medical Association, by William E. Steslicke. New York: Praeger, 1973.

The Japan Teachers Union: A Radical Interest Group in Japanese Politics, by Donald Ray Thurston. Princeton: Princeton University Press, 1973.

Japan's Foreign Policy, 1868-1941: A Research Guide, edited by James William Morley. New York: Columbia University Press, 1974.

Palace and Politics in Prewar Japan, by David Anson Titus. New York: Columbia University Press, 1974.

The Idea of China: Essays in Geographic Myth and Theory, by Andrew March. Devon, England: David and Charles, 1974.

Origins of the Cultural Revolution, by Roderick MacFarquhar. New York: Columbia University Press, 1974.

Shiba Kokan: Artist, Innovator, and Pioneer in the Westernization of Japan, by Calvin L. French. Tokyo: Weatherhill, 1974.

Insei: Abdicated Sovereigns in the Politics of Late Heian Japan, by G. Cameron Hurst. New York: Columbia University Press, 1975.

Embassy at War, by Harold Joyce Noble. Edited with an introduction by Frank Baldwin, Jr. Seattle: University of Washington Press, 1975.

Rebels and Bureaucrats: China's December 9ers, by John Israel and Donald W. Klein. Berkeley: University of California Press, 1975.

Deterrent Diplomacy, edited by James William Morley. New York: Columbia University Press, 1976.

House United, House Divided: The Chinese Family in Taiwan, by Myron L. Cohen. New York: Columbia University Press, 1976.

Escape from Predicament: Neo-Confucianism and China's Evolving Political Culture, by Thomas A. Metzger. New York: Columbia University Press, 1976.

Cadres, Commanders, and Commissars: The Training of the Chinese Communist Leadership, 1920-45, by Jane L. Price. Boulder, Colo.: Westview Press, 1976.

Sun Yat-sen: Frustrated Patriot, by C. Martin Wilbur. New York: Columbia University Press, 1977.

Japanese International Negotiating Style, by Michael Blaker. New York: Columbia University Press, 1977.

Contemporary Japanese Budget Politics, by John Creighton Campbell. Berkeley: University of California Press, 1977.

The Medieval Chinese Oligarchy, by David Johnson. Boulder, Colo.: Westview Press, 1977.

The Arms of Kiangnan: Modernization in the Chinese Ordnance Industry, 1860-1895, by Thomas L. Kennedy. Boulder, Colo.: Westview Press, 1978.

Patterns of Japanese Policymaking: Experiences from Higher Education, by T. J. Pempel. Boulder, Colo.: Westview Press, 1978.

The Chinese Connection: Roger S. Greene, Thomas W. Lamont, George E. Sokolsky, and American-East Asian Relations, by Warren I. Cohen. New York: Columbia University Press, 1978.

Militarism in Modern China: The Career of Wu P'ei-fu, 1916-1939, by Odoric Y. K. Wou. Folkestone, England: Dawson, 1978.

A Chinese Pioneer Family: The Lins of Wu-feng, by Johanna Meskill. Princeton: Princeton University Press, 1979.

Perspectives on a Changing China, edited by Joshua A. Fogel and William T. Rowe. Boulder, Colo.: Westview Press, 1979.

The Memoirs of Li Tsung-jen, by T. K. Tong and Li Tsung-jen. Boulder, Colo.: Westview Press, 1979.

Unwelcome Muse: Chinese Literature in Shanghai and Peking, 1937-1945, by Edward Gunn. New York: Columbia University Press, 1979.

Yenan and the Great Powers, by James Reardon-Anderson. New York: Columbia University Press, 1980.

Uncertain Years: Chinese-American Relations, 1947-1950, edited by Dorothy Borg and Waldo Heinrichs. New York: Columbia University Press, 1980.

The Fateful Choice: Japan's Advance into Southeast Asia, edited by James William Morley. New York: Columbia University Press, 1980.

Tanaka Giichi and Japan's China Policy, by William F. Morton. Folkestone, England: Dawson, 1980; New York: St. Martin's Press, 1980.

The Origins of the Korean War: Liberation and the Emergence of Separate Regimes, 1945-1947, by Bruce Cumings. Princeton: Princeton University Press, 1981.

Class Conflict in Chinese Socialism, by Richard Curt Kraus. New York: Columbia University Press, 1981.

Education Under Mao: Class and Competition in Canton Schools, by Jonathan Unger. New York: Columbia University Press, 1982.

Japan and the San Francisco Peace Settlement, by Michael M. Yoshitsu. New York: Columbia University Press, 1982.